THE COMPLETE GUIDE TO

DEVELOPING COMMERCIAL REAL ESTATE

The Who, What, Where, Why and How
PRINCIPLES of DEVELOPING
COMMERCIAL REAL ESTATE

ROBERT A. WEHRMEYER

Copyright © 2010, 2013 by Wehr Ventures
All Rights Reserved
Printed in the United States of America
Published by Wehr Publishing
San Antonio, Texas 78015

ISBN: 0-9845346-0-1
ISBN-13: 978-0-9845346-0-9
LCCN: 2010916762

To order additional copies of this book, please visit www.wehrventures.com and www.developingcre.com

WehrVentures
dba for Otali Solutions, LLC

ABOUT THE AUTHOR

Mr. Wehrmeyer is a lawyer and commercial real estate developer who specializes in health care related development projects. A recent project, developed by Mr. Wehrmeyer and the development team was selected as the Office Building of the Year in San Antonio, Texas. Now living in San Antonio, Mr. Wehrmeyer and his wife of more than twenty years, Cindy, have two children, daughter, Ashley, and son, Trey.

ACKNOWLEDGMENTS

I would like to thank Clint Holland and Scott Boynton for assistance with graphs, budgets, templates, and general review of the financial sections. I am indebted to Noemi Skok for her relentless editorializing of life and outline. Special thanks to Judge Glen Ayers who was, in large part, the inspiration behind my life goal to write a book and teach at the college level. Finally, to my brother Mike who was instrumental in helping me navigate the publishing world of image pixilation, compression, resolution, distillation and DPI, his patience, insight and wisdom is only exceeded by his years.

Much gratitude and love to my wife, Cindy, daughter, Ashley, and son, Trey, for their support and generally putting up with me over the years.

TABLE OF CONTENTS

Getting the Tenant to Sign a Lease Agreement

Tenant Lease Guarantee

The Letter of Intent: Basic LOI Terms

Owner Occupied Tenants

Trends in Real Estate Development: Integrated Project Delivery

PART 2: THE WHAT PRINCIPLE

Introduction: General Phases of Commercial Real Estate Development

Vision and Predevelopment

    Predevelopment Phase Expenses

    Transition: Predevelopment to Construction

Construction Phase

    The General Contractor and Initial Construction

    The Developer Role during Construction

    Tenant Build Out and Construction

    Competitively Bidding Out Tenant Improvement

Management and Operations Phase

    Developer Managed and Operated Buildings

Sale or Refinance Phase

    Why Buy a Stabilized Building

    Selling the Project

Predevelopment: City Planning Land Development Office

Property Acquisition: Contract to Purchase Land

Purchasing the Land versus Financing the Project

Trends in Real Estate Development: Green Building, LEED Certification, and Sustainability..

PART 3: THE WHERE PRINCIPLE

Introduction

General Area Analysis

Target Area Analysis

Specific Use Analysis

Demographic Research

Sources of Information

PART 4: THE WHY PRINCIPLE

Why Is the Project Going to Succeed?

Introduction

Land Cost

Hard Costs

Soft Costs

Tenant Improvement Costs

Financing Incremental Tenant Improvement Costs

Financing and Interest Costs

Budget Overruns

How to Determine an Appropriate Lease Rate

Operating Pro Forma

Tenant Load Factor and Rentable versus Usable Square Footage

Long-Term Debt Financing: Sale or Refinancing

Hold Period

Profit Assumptions

Profit Analysis, Discounted Cash Flow, and Cap Rates

Waterfall Distribution of Profits and Summary Financials

Introduction

Key Components of a Project Plan

PART 5: THE HOW PRINCIPLE

How to Get the Project Financed and Built: Why Read the Last Chapter First?

Introduction

Loan Process

Project Appraisal

Construction Loan

Developer Fee

Tenants and the Importance of Preleasing

Debt Service Coverage and Interest Coverage Ratio

Government Enhancement Programs

One-Stop-Shop Financing Alternatives

Lenders' Legal Structure

Construction Draw or Funding Process

Land Financing

Land as Equity

The Master Site Plan and Multiple Phases

Selling Pad Sites

Purchasing and Refurbishing an Existing Building

Construction Loan and Marketing Basics

Introduction

Equity Investment Process

The Equity Investor and Return on Investment

ROI, IRR, and the Time Value of Money

The Developer Coinvestment

Developer Fee Caveats

The Developer as Tenant

Mezzanine Financing

The Equity Investor Legal Structure

The Equity Investor Underwriting Criteria

THE PROJECT VISION

INTRODUCTION

THE PROJECT VISION

Every new development project whether a hospital, retail center, hotel, or apartment complex starts with someone who has the insight, drive, and passion to try something new. It takes someone with vision.

Developers do all this and more—but how? How do developers turn vacant lots into successful community developments?

This outline will explore not only the how but the principles of who, what, where and why of commercial real estate development (CRE) and guide the reader through the process of developers converting their vision into actual functioning projects.

From the developer's perspective the well-known golden rule of real estate, location, location, location—might well be changed to finance, finance, finance. If a developer can finance a project, he can get it built. Getting financing therefore becomes the single biggest obstacle to moving from the developer's vision, to construction, to completion, and finally to an open, operating, and successful development.

The who, what, where, why, and how guide to developing commercial real estate is based on the premise that obtaining financing for a new development project will force the developer to ask and answer all the critical questions that must be asked and answered in order to justify and succeed in getting a new project built.

The who, what, and where chapters of this book address the key components of the developer's vision. These components are:

"What is the developer going to build, where is the developer plannng to build, and who is the developer building it for?"

Once you have asked and answered all of the key questions associated with the developer's vision (the who, what, and where), you have all the basic information needed to address the commercial real estate principle of why will the project be a success?

The why chapter of the book is where all the key components addressed in the who, what, and where chapters come together to justify why the project should be built and results in a detailed *project plan and financial analysis.*

Throughout this guide we will use a hypothetical development project of a **sports bar and restaurant** to address what must be asked and answered about a proposed development project.

Once all of the key components set forth in the who, what, where, and why principles are answered, we will address the how principle. How do you make the sports bar and restaurant a reality? How does a developer convert a vision for a restaurant sports bar, hotel, strip center, apartment complex, or medical facility into a real project that is open to and serving the community?

WHO SHOULD READ THIS BOOK

If you are new to developing commercial real estate, this book will guide you through each material stage of development and help you ask and answer the key questions that must be considered. If you are experienced in real estate project development, this guide can help you in areas where you may not have had as much experience or exposure as you would like before you commit the time, money, and energy required. For example, many contractors want to develop a piece of property but may not be as versed in how to raise the equity portion needed to finance a development project. A real estate broker who has worked on numerous development efforts may feel he understands the financing but may not be comfortable with some of the legal issues and enterprise requirements. Of course, everyone who is thinking about developing real estate will want to know about the personal exposure and liability and what the economic and personal rewards should be!

Whatever the question, issue, or concern this book is set up to help the reader ask and answer the key questions that must be asked and answered to evaluate, analyze and actually create a new real estate development project.

HOW TO READ THIS BOOK

Read the how section first!

As stated earlier, location, location, location, the real estate mantra, might well be translated to *finance, finance, finance*. Barring a personal fortune or a rich parent or relative, getting the financing, investment, or cash needed to develop a commercial real estate project determines the entire process of the who, what, where, why, and how *principles* to get a project built.

This book is based on the theory that meeting the needs and demands of potential financing partners will force the novice or experienced developer to ask and answer all of the critical questions to move a new CRE development project forward. Getting someone to finance a project with both *debt and equity,* which is sometimes referred to as the *capital stack,* addresses most if not all of the critical questions that need to be asked and answered to put a project on the right path for success.

That is why we recommend reading the section on how to get the project financed and built first! Reading the last chapter first will give the reader an introduction to the basic principles behind the who, what, where, and why principles of the book.

Look for this arrow ➡ throughout the who, what, where, why, and how principles discussion; it will indicate important issues or concepts.

PREFACE

When I started developing real estate it quickly became apparent that while I would look at lot of potential deals, there were few successes. It also became apparent that I needed a way to screen the numerous opportunities and focus on those projects with the best chance for success. Moreover, I came to realize that reaching the goal of closing a construction loan for a project was the most important step in a new development project becoming a reality. With the closing of the construction loan, a project moves from the stage of hoping to be built to a high likelihood it will be built. Therefore, I settled on the premise that if a real estate development project appeared to be finance-able, it was worth taking a closer look.

That being said, financing for a development project is not always easy to identify and close. It is not uncommon for a developer to approach multiple sources and attempt many times to obtain and close financing for a project. It can take years to arrange and close acceptable financing. Do not interpret this to mean that financing can or should determine whether or not the project you want to create is a good one to develop. Financing is merely a very important tool to assist the developer in asking and answering the right questions to evaluate a project's potential.

Finally, this is not a book about real estate finance. I am a lawyer turned developer and have no prior real estate finance experience. However, the financial aspects of developing real estate are important and a high priority when it comes to raising investment capital and convincing others the project is a good one. Therefore, it is important to understand certain fundamental concepts related to real estate finance. Since these concepts were written by a nonfinancial person (me), I hope that you will find them easy to understand.

PART 1:
THE WHO PRINCIPLE
WHO ARE YOU DEVELOPING AND BUILDING THE PROJECT FOR?

In this section:

Who are the developer, the development team, and actual and anticipated tenants and users?

CHAPTER 1: WHO IS THE DEVELOPER?

INTRODUCTION

As the developer, you are the main force behind the promotion of the project and are responsible for leading each and every aspect of the project's success. The lenders/investors, team members, and partners will look to you for leadership, strength, promotion, knowledge, and experience related to the development project. ➡ Do not underestimate the power of the personality and confidence of the developer in getting a lender or equity investor to invest in the project and convincing team members to join the team. It is often the dividing line between yes and no. Donald Trump, Walt Disney, and now even Jerry Jones of the Dallas Cowboys illustrate the power of personality behind extraordinary development efforts.

1 DEVELOPER RESPONSIBILITY: A SENSE OF COMMUNITY

Every commercial real estate development effort, no matter how large or small has some impact on the surrounding neighborhood, local community, and environment. Let us examine the restaurant and sports bar we will use as a guide throughout this book. Most people have enjoyed having dinner, visiting with friends, and watching their favorite team at a local restaurant and sports bar. However many sports bars draw large, often loud crowds and can be open late into the evening or early morning. As the developer, it is incumbent on you to examine the impact the planned development may have on the local and surrounding community. If, for example, one of the sites being reviewed for the sports bar and restaurant development is adjacent to a family-oriented neighborhood, grade school, and or church, it is wise to be proactive and discuss the planned development with community leaders and those living and working closest to the site. In fact, many jurisdictions will greatly restrict certain businesses close to churches, schools, and local neighborhoods–especially businesses serving alcohol. Another method developers can utilize to create a sense of community is LID or low impact development. LID is an approach to development that incorporates many natural or existing features from the site into the development effort. A LID oriented development may attempt to manage storm water by utilizing the natural storm water source, limiting *impervious cover* (think parking lot) and maintaining natural landscape features. In any event, regardless of jurisdiction, zoning or regulatory restrictions, and requirements, a developer must take responsibility for the impact the proposed development may have on the community. Examine and evaluate these issues early in the development and make a sense of community an important part of the project goals and objectives. We will examine specific development issues, environmental impact, project *sustainability*, and *LEED certification* in the what section of the book.

Put yourself in the shoes of the lender or equity investor and consider what he might be thinking in reviewing a request for a real estate loan or investment.

As the lender or investor, you know that you have a limited amount of money to invest and a limited window of opportunity to make the investment and ultimately realize a return on the invested money. You, as the lender or investor, will most likely want to invest in a project that involves an experienced developer and an experienced development team in a project type that has a proven track record of success in the market where it is being built. In other words, the lender/investor wants the best possible return for the least amount of risk!

Keeping this role reversal in mind consider what you must do to convince the lender/ investor that the CRE development project you are proposing should be the project of choice and is worthy of his time, attention, and money. First, the developer needs to address certain *business basics*.

2 BUSINESS PLAN AND SUMMARY

The business basics start with a business plan, a project plan, and budget. (More on the project plan and budget in the why section of this book.) The business plan is one of the first steps in addressing the key question who is the developer? That question is an important business basic.

The business plan is an opportunity to demonstrate to the potential investors and others that the developer has adequately thought out his business goals and objectives, and can clearly translate these goals and objectives into an attractive plan and development opportunities. The business plan is a chance for the developer to demonstrate strengths and anticipate and explain weaknesses. Finally, it represents a chance to package these qualities in such a way that they are simple to understand and appreciate. A good business plan and summary will help lead the lender/investor to a keen understanding of who you are and what you are doing. Most importantly, it can pique the interest of a potential investor who will want to hear more about the project plan.

A business plan can be presented in an infinite number of ways but a basic business plan should attempt to address each of the following key components: *business strategy, target market and analysis, business goals and objectives, and finally certain specifics about the developer and team,* including *background, experience, pipeline of business, and personal and business references.*

If we continue to leverage the sports bar and restaurant concept referred to earlier, we can show how each of these components could be addressed. To apply the sports bar and restaurant concept, we have to make certain assumptions. First, we will assume the owner of the restaurant has told you he wants to focus on the operations and therefore is looking to you to develop the real estate. The tenant, the restaurant operator, wants to incorporate certain aspects into the first store that are associated with the *brand* that he incorporated into his original store. The sports bar and restaurant owner has also informed you that he plans on expanding in five additional major markets in the state in the next year and want each location to be near a college. You have been busy identifying potential locations within these markets with a population base that is low to middle income, high growth, and near a local college—the target market. So the business strategy is to leverage the brand and to do this in a location that can also take advantage of the local college and surrounding population. The business objective is to leverage one store that utilizes the brand developed in the initial store and to grow this concept into numerous stores in numerous markets over the next year. Now, add personal and business background of the team partners, experience, and references, and you have the basic tenets of a good business plan.

One final note on the business plan described above: like many aspects of what we will address in this book, there are hundreds of approaches and examples of good business plans.

We will only touch on one approach. A simple search on the Internet will yield numerous approaches and examples. Once the developer has a basic business plan he believes in and is excited about, the developer will want to make sure it is flexible enough to adapt to the debt and equity investors that might be interested in the development effort. Understanding the target investment audience and what will be attractive to them is extremely important. For example, you may want to raise equity from a local investor before you attempt to raise the money necessary to expand the concept to other markets. The local investor might only have the resources for the first real estate project but might be attracted to the potential of being a part of a larger growth strategy. Conversely, larger institutional equity investors are likely to be more interested in investing the capital needed to expand an existing concept that is successful in more than one market (see the risk reward discussion addressed in the how chapter.) Customize the presentation to suit the needs of the investment group but maintain the integrity of the business plan, strategy, and objectives.

Finally, the business plan and day-to-day communication will incorporate certain fundamental business basics. It is often assumed that the business basics have been addressed when they tend to be overlooked or addressed in a haphazard way until they are missed. Then they become highlighted questions marks that raise doubt in the minds of the potential investor. It is better to address these simple issues up front and get right to selling the project plan.

3 COMPANY STRUCTURE: CORPORATE, COMPANY, AND WEB NAME

Most lenders and equity providers expect and even assume that certain fundamental business basics are already in place before considering an investment project. Let us try the role reversal once again. The investor receives written correspondence as a follow-up to a meeting with you, the developer. The letter (or e-mail) does not arrive on letterhead, has no corporate name or logo, and gives a Post Office box for the business address. The developer requests that you respond to a commercial third party e-mail address and doesn't provide a company e-mail or Web address.

As the potential investor you might begin to wonder with whom you are dealing? These types of concerns may not be determinative but can often be damaging to the recipient's opinion of you and the proposed project investment. There is, however, no reason for the issues to be a concern to the potential investors. Get the fundamental business basics in place, and you can diffuse any perception problems and get right to focusing on the vision and project plan.

4 ENTERPRISE LEGAL STRUCTURES

One material fundamental business basic is choosing the developer's enterprise legal structure. Most developers, sooner or later, will form a legal entity from which they will represent their enterprise. The entity choices are typically *sole proprietorship, corporation, limited liability company, general partnership or limited partnership*. A sole proprietorship is merely a business run and operated through you as an individual and makes no distinction between personal assets and business assets. Some states recognize the concept of a *general partnership*. A general partnership is one where each partner has unlimited liability. A *corporation* is a traditional corporate structure and is treated as if the entity is a "person" in and of itself, separate and distinct from the developer. If run properly, the traditional corporate structure offers the developer the most protective structure or what is sometimes referred to as the *corporate veil*. The corporate veil is the phase often used by lawyers to describe how the law separates you as a person from exposure or problems that may arise because of something that happened as a result of the business operation. Run properly, the corporation and the corporate veil can rarely be pierced by lawsuit or other liability. Of course, the corporate structure offers other benefits besides liability protection such as ease of ownership transfer, accommodation of multiple owners, separate bank credit, and survival after the death of a shareholder. One downside to the corporate structure is double taxation—a corporation pays tax on revenues, and its shareholders can pay tax again on distributions.

Another twist to the corporate vehicle is the *limited liability company or LLC*. Most states have provisions that allow for the LLC structure. A limited liability company is a unique mixture of the benefits of a corporation, including the corporate veil, and the ease and simplicity of a sole proprietorship. The LLC allows you to form a company but be treated for certain purposes as a sole proprietorship. There are members rather than shareholders and no minutes or resolutions are required. Moreover while the LLC consists of a legitimate corporate-type structure, it is taxed to you personally, and you are not held liable for the debts or liabilities of the company unless you agree to this in some form of guarantee. The LLC corporate concept, at least in part, was created as a way to encourage small business growth and investment. It remains a valuable vehicle and is often the vehicle of choice for development company entities.

The *Limited Partnership or LP entity* is also common amongst development companies but for different reasons, as we will discuss in the *how* chapter. Equity investors like the LP enterprise structure when they decide to make an investment in a project. The reason for this is found in the name—limited partnership. The basic distinction of a limited partnership or LP is to encourage investment by investors but to limit their personal exposure to any liability to their investment amount. Much like a shareholders liability is limited to his investment in corporate shares. If equity investor A invests one million dollars in a project and a catastrophic event occurs, causing the project to collapse in one big lawsuit, investor A can only lose the one million dollar investment. The investor loss exposure in our example, although significant in dollar amount, is limited. At least that's the plan. Lawyers have been chipping away at the LP armor (and corporate armor) for years. However, limiting loss exposure or liability comes at a price. The price investor A must pay for this limited liability is control and the passive nature of the investment. The law allows the limited liability only if equity investor A maintains a limited role in the investment enterprise. The logic being that if the role is limited to just investing, the investor shouldn't be held liable for poor judgment or management by the people running the project. Therefore, in a limited partnership the limited partners get together and select a *general partner or GP*. The GP will own a small piece of the LP and is charged with active management and governance of the operations and project venture. The good news is that the developer is normally in charge of the GP, the day-to-day decisions of the partnership, and therefore the project. Equity investors however, have found ways to control many of the material functions of the GP, and these controls are typically set forth in the formal *partnership agreement*. However, for the developer, being the GP of the limited partnership with the equity investors is still very important to maintaining control over the vision and project plan.

Finally, the company entity, whether sole proprietorship, corporation, limited liability, company, or limited partnership is the organization that will legally identify and define your business. This new entity is registered with the state you wish to incorporate in by filing the appropriate corporate, company, or partnership documents with the *secretary of state's* office. (To locate the Web site for your state's secretary of state, use www.sos.stateXXXX.org [insert the state name in place of XXXX].

5 BRANDING AND FUNDAMENTAL BUSINESS BASICS

In today's world, the presentation of the business basics by the developer to investors and others has changed dramatically. The Internet is now the single most powerful tool to communicate to the world who you are and what you do. However, traditional communication and marketing tools are still very important and hard copy brochures, letterhead, and other fundamental business basics remain very important in presenting the developer and project plan. However, fundamental business basics must now be incorporated not only into traditional hard copy media but also into the digital technology, Web domain, and other Web media options.

With this in mind, let's use the traditional letterhead as a form of poster board to outline the fundamental business basics. First and typically most prominent on our letterhead poster board is the *company name, logo, and tag line.* This can be the same as or different than the corporate enterprise name, but it is essentially the name you want customers and stakeholders to remember and identify with the business or project. A quick search on the Internet will often let you know if the desired name is available and not being used by a similar business. The key term here is *similar business.* You may still be able to use a name even if someone else is already using it if it is being used in an unrelated industry and an overlap of customers and business operations is unlikely. The business name is often associated with a *logo* and is often *trademarked.* Creating a business logo that can be used as a trademark can be invaluable. The logo is typically a visual tool to create an image around the company name and create a form of association with the product, service, or image.

Enterprise, Dot-Com, and Trademark Names:

It is important to understand that the ➡ enterprise entity (business name), dot-com name, and the trademark name are three separate and distinct names and assets. All three require certain actions on the part of the developer to secure any rights to use. For example the corporate name will be embodied in a document like an articles of incorporation and filed with the secretary of state's office in the state where you decide to incorporate. The dot-com name, Web site, etc. will be perfected by registering with a domain service; the trademark can be registered and perfected by filing with the U.S. Patent and Trademark Office (or appropriate office in another country). Trademarks actually become a little trickier in that you start to acquire the right to the name or service when you begin to use it. See the project, teaming partner, and legal counsel for more information. In any event, having a name that you like requires that you juggle all three approaches—enterprise name, dot-com name, and trademark name. ➥ Use and approval for one purpose does not secure the right to the use for one of the other purposes.

To continue with our letterhead example, traditionally, the letterhead is where the reader will find basic contact information for the company. Of course, this has also changed dramatically. Along with street address, phone and fax numbers, you can now add information for the Web site, e-mail address, and social networking sites. One final point, if you can't afford office space, set up a street address with one of the postal service commercial businesses instead of using a Post Office box. A street address gives impression of substance and overnight mail can be difficult to deliver to a Post Office box address.

You are likely to want the business name and domain name to be similar if not identical. However, almost everyone has experienced how difficult it can be to get the domain name you want. Since you are putting together a business plan and summary for investors for the development business the developer can always resort to using the personal name or initials in the dot-com. In any event, matching up the business name and the dot-com name isn't always easy, but a Web address and Web site that can easily be associated with the development company is an essential and fundamental business basic. Many developers today will create a separate Web site for each project they are developing or create a separate Web page on the developer Web site.

When you register with a domain service, you will also get e-mail address options associated with the Web address and access to blogs and social networking sites. Business e-mail associated with a Web site is not only a great first marketing tool but operates as a fundamental basic business for an investor's review of you, the business plan, and proposed project plan.

6 FINANCIAL AND MANAGEMENT SOFTWARE

One additional tool to invest in early is a way to manage internal accounting. A financial reporting and accounting software will help forecast project financials; keep track of expenses, revenue, and taxes; and make it possible to keep up with all of the financial reporting requirements required by the debt and equity as a part of the construction loan and equity investment. Personal guarantees require periodic (usually no less than quarterly) financial statement disclosure. It can also be beneficial to have a financial reporting system that would allow you to demonstrate to the construction lender or equity investor that you can manage not only internal business affairs but the construction loan draw process as well. As described in the what section of this book, construction loans work on a monthly request for funds, and the developer needs to oversee and typically administer the predevelopment draw process. *Draw management* is another good reason to invest in appropriate business management software. Finally, if you want to manage the development project operations upon completion of construction you will need or want software to help you report on the numerous aspects of the project operations and performance.

Chapter 2: WHO Means the Project Teaming Partners

INTRODUCTION

Commercial Real Estate developers have perfected the art of bringing together various professionals and presenting the group as a team. The team can then present its credentials as one entity to help close a construction loan, convince an equity investor to invest, or to bid on a *request for proposal (RFP)*. An RFP is a written request that sets forth specifics for a development construction project and asks interested developers and teams to respond by bidding on the work.

If you ➡ are a novice real estate developer, you can leverage the experience of the team to demonstrate to the lender, equity provider, RFP solicitor, tenants, and others the probable success of the proposed project. If you are an experienced developer, you can leverage the experience of the team to demonstrate the probable success of the proposed project—sound familiar? In almost every instance the developer will want to add to the project plan the experience, *past performance,* and comparable projects of the chosen teaming partners. This information will be very important to potential lenders, equity investors, and entities soliciting RFPs, as well as others, in demonstrating the experience and know-how of each member of the project team.

1 TEAMING PARTNERS

You cannot be an expert in each and every phase of a commercial real estate development, but a good developer will find competent professionals with the necessary expertise to form a team with him to help the project succeed. The ability to assemble the right team is paramount in demonstrating to the construction lender and equity investor, potential tenants, and others that you have assembled the key players necessary to create a successful development.

Here is a general summary of the key professionals involved in a typical development project:

Architects: The project vision is first translated to something visual and understandable by the architect; he will attempt to draw the vision and project plan. The architects will draw the vision with such detail that the design will literally take up hundreds of very large pages. The document or drawings they produce are referred to as the *architectural plans and specifications* sometimes referred to as the *"drawings"* for the project. Most architectural firms specialize in certain types of development projects. It is helpful to find an architect who has specific experience in the planned development product type, the planned location, and tenant type. His experience will be invaluable in presenting the project plan to the lender, equity investor, potential tenants, and other teaming partners. Before you approve the architect to move forward with the final plans and specs, you want to make sure the project is well on its way to being financeable. Final drawings from the architect can cost tens of thousands and even hundreds of thousands of dollars, and architects expect to get paid whether the construction loan closes or not.

Before the creation of the plans and specs and early in the development process you will want the architect to draw the vision. The initial drawings by the architect that you should request are called the *site plan and rendering*. The site plan is important because it shows how the project outline might look superimposed on the chosen site. The *rendering* is important because it is a graphic demonstration of project vision. The architect can also create an *elevation*. An elevation is a representation or façade of one view of the building or buildings. You will also want to enter into a written agreement with the architect early on in the process. The American Institute of Architects (AIA) has many forms you can use, depending on the size, project type, and other factors. The AIA Web site (www. aia. org) is a good source, it's important to bear in mind that AIA forms are not written from the perspective of the owner/developer. As may be obvious, the AIA forms are written from the perspective of the architect. For example many developers believe once they pay the architect they own and have the rights to the drawings. This may not be the case. The AIA may specify that the intellectual property is owned by the architect. To secure these rights and others the developer should carefully review the AIA with the team legal counsel and specify in the agreement that the developer has a right to a nonexclusive license to use the intellectual property or *instruments of service* and to an electronic copy or *com-*

puter aided design or CAD copy of the files. There are organizations constantly reviewing and commenting to the various forms and recommending modifications and changes. A simple internet search by the developer is an easy way to find and review these comments. Ultimately, the AIA form or equivalent contract form will need to be executed and will be an expected part of the diligence of the lender and equity investors.

Another key player in the development process that is often associated with the architect is the *commercial interior designer.* In most jurisdictions commercial interior designers are licensed professionals and can play a key role in all phases of a typical commercial development. A design professional can assist in initial programming, design (both schematic and development), and implementation. Most designers will work with not only the developer on the interior of the core and shell of the project but with each of the tenants for the project. Meaning they will assist the developer (and tenants) with interior floor planning, space planning, budgeting, selection of finished materials, furnishings, and equipment, as well as timing associated with the ordering, delivery, and installation of the above while coordinating these events with the construction and architectural professionals.

General Contractor and Construction Manager: Most construction projects are based on a *design-bid-build* approach. The design-bid-build approach merely refers to the fact that the architect will design the project, with the design in hand the developer and the architect will bid out the project to select a GC and once selected the GC will build the project the architect has designed. The process of selecting and picking the right GC can go a long way in convincing the lender and equity investor that you have the experience and know-how to bring the planned project to completion. The *general contractor* or *GC* and or *construction manager* or *CM* is the entity that enters into a contract with the developer for the purpose of construction of the project. The two terms are often used interchangeably however a CM is most often distinguished from the GC in that a CM will provide pre-construction services and most often used when a project is considered complex or time for completion is limited.

The GC or CM is often considered the quarterback of the construction team and process. The GC is responsible for organization of the entire construction team, schedule, safety, and all processes that lead to a completed building. The GC will establish a responsibility matrix, milestone schedule, site utilization plan, construction documents, bid and choose the subs, manage each discipline, bid purchase, coordinate delivery and installation of equipment and supplies, and incorporate all of these in the overall construction scheme and schedule. Of course, from the perspective of the developer this activity by the GC should result in a completed building(s) and project built to the plans and specifications established by the architect.

The GC has been hired to build what the architect has set forth in the plans and specifications for the project—no more and certainly no less. However, you can ask the GC to do a review of what and how the architect has set forth the vision in the plans and specs. This review process is often referred to as *value engineering* and can be, as the name suggests, very valuable. A GC will often bring a more practical insight to what is being built and can save you thousands if not tens of thousands of dollars. However value engineering is not just changing architectural plans of the vision. Value engineering can have a significant impact on the building's performance, especially in the mechanical, electrical, and plumbing areas.

There are a couple of basic contractual approaches to engaging a GC. There are many applicable AIA forms and there is an AIA owner form for cases in which the general contractor is the constructor. Again, keep in mind that these forms were not written with the best interest of the owner/developer in mind. For example, the AIA forms typically will not include milestone dates for substantial completion and will rarely list financial damages if the GC is responsible for substantial delay in the construction schedule. The standard AIA form actually goes a step further and waives recovery of consequential damage. It is important to get the development team legal counsel involved early in discussing the terms and conditions of contracting with the GC or CM.

There are numerous ways to contract for the GC services. A GC can be engaged to construct a project on a *stipulated sum or lump sum basis,* which means the contractor will estimate the total cost of the construction services, add an acceptable profit and overhead charge (typically, 10-18% of the project cost) and the developer agrees to pay this amount. If the project cost turns out to be greater than what the GC estimates the GC profit is reduced. If costs are less than the GC estimated then the GC can actually make more profit. Often this method is used by the developer to incent the GC to look for ways to save costs during the construction process. The stipulated sum or lump sum approach is often associated with the design-build-bid construction method. A GC or CM can also be engaged to construct a project on a *cost plus* basis. A cost plus contractual relationship means the cost of the work plus a fixed fee. No additional profit based on cost savings can be achieved. The developer can carry this concept a step further by utilizing the *Guaranteed Maximum Price* or GMP contractual approach. In the GMP or G-MAX approach the CM and the developer agree that total construction cost will not exceed a certain amount. The CM is at risk for the cost overruns that might occur during the construction process and not approved by the developer. There is also a *design build contract,* which is an approach that allows one company or entity to perform the architectural, engineering, and contracting for the project. The lender and the equity investor will often have a preference for the contract type with the GC and more often than not prefer contracts that shift the burden or risk to the GC when there are unjustified cost overruns (See GMP or G-MAX).

Financial Analyst: If staying up late creating numerical fields and running numbers through a spreadsheet is not your idea of a good time, early in the development process find a *financial analyst* who enjoys number crunching at this level to join the team. Preferably, of course, one who understands and knows real estate and real estate finance. This person is truly invaluable. This person will and must understand the project, the market, and the key players; he can help you express the whole scope of the project in language the lender and equity providers will not only understand but will demand from you....repeatedly. You will be constantly changing, massaging, and editing the project plan, budget, financing analysis, and profit analysis to fit the needs and desires of the project investors.

Engineers: There is an *engineer* involved in every aspect of a commercial development project. Specific types of engineers get involved in every aspect of the process from plotting out the utilities, to surveying the property, to assessing soils and environmental problems, to analyzing topography, to controlling dust, to assessing off- and on-site issues, helping with the building's construction, tenant improvement issues—all aspects of the development. While engineers may seem prolific in the development process, they are extremely important and one of the most valuable resources for information and certainly for performing essential required functions. If you utilize an out-of-town contractor and/or architect, consider utilizing the local engineering pool. Engineers are often the most versed and experienced of the team members in dealing with the applicable city permit and other regulatory authorities. Remember you cannot build without a *permit,* and the longer it takes you to get a permit, the more at risk the project becomes. Here is a short list of some of the different engineers utilized in a new construction project: *civil engineers, surveyors, cost engineers, mechanical engineers, electrical engineers, structural engineers, fire protection engineers, and environmental engineers.* You will need to engage an engineer early in the process to survey the property. A survey is needed to assist the architect in understanding the site and how the buildings for the project will fit into the site, based on the issues disclosed in the survey. For example, if there is an easement located on the site, you may not be able to build on or near the easement. An *easement* is an interest in the property that is held by someone else other than the land owner that authorizes the use of that property for a specific purpose. The survey conducted by the engineers will identify easements and other issues and help the architect design the building(s) in the appropriate location on the site. In fact most architects will want the ALTA survey, topographic survey, utilities survey and tree survey (assuming these surveys exist) to do the initial site assessment.

Other Developers: Local developers can be good teaming partners because they know the local playing field. They often know the process with the city regulators and officials, and they know the key engineers and other key local potential teaming partners for the project. They may also know potential tenants for the project. If you are the local developer, teaming with a national developer can help you bring financial muscle, attract experienced teaming partners, solidify interest from lender and equity investor, and they may represent an opportunity to share the *developer net worth covenants,* as well as the guarantees and indemnities, with a deeper pocket.

Real Estate Brokers: As you may have already realized, finding an experienced, qualified broker for the property type and location is extremely important. The real estate broker will assist you with numerous functions from finding potential tenants to tracking *sales comps, lease rates, absorption statistics,* and other market trends. However, engaging a qualified broker who is knowledgeable in the appropriate product type and location is only part of the solution for finding tenants to occupy the project. Brokers make a living bringing tenants and landlords together. This means they have other projects, other clients, and other priorities. You, on the other hand, are highly unlikely to get the vision and project plan off the ground unless you can demonstrate that sufficient tenants are committed or will commit to the project. This means that you, not the broker, are primarily responsible for getting tenants committed. Finally, brokers are not always versed in the struggles and demands developer faces when he attempts to procure financing. Brokers, for example, do not always understand the need to get a signed lease agreement from a tenant rather than just the letter of intent (LOI).

Typically, the developer and broker will enter into a *listing agreement* for leasing and or the leasing and sale of the project. This agreement will, amongst other things, outline the owner's responsibilities and the broker's duties and commission structure and the agreement can be exclusive or non-exclusive. It is a good idea to interview numerous brokers to make sure you know the market approach for broker duties and commissions. There are different standards on how commissions are calculated and paid. For example, in some areas the commission is based on gross rental revenue, which may include the triple net expense pass through revenue. In addition you will probably be responsible for paying the tenant representative, as well as the broker you have hired. Finally, it is typical in most markets to pay half of the commission earned upon signing the lease agreement and the remaining half upon occupancy. You will need to know all of this information to accurately budget for this area of the project expense; we'll learn more about this in the why chapter of the book. Interviewing numerous brokers will give you more experience in the market and greater exposure to market-driven leasing terms, including commission, and understanding of how they are calculated and paid.

In any event, the experienced local broker will be invaluable in helping introduce you to potential tenants, other brokers, understanding the local market demographics, commission structures, comparable leasing product, and marketing the project; more about this in the where section of the book.

Bankers: In many instances the CRE construction loan is the bread and butter of the community bank lender. Believe it or not some lenders actually like discussing potential projects with developers. It can be refreshing to actually present to someone that will take the time to listen to the vision and project plan. That being said, most bankers, lenders, and even equity investors doing construction loans and investments tend to specialize or favor lending for specific product types. Therefore, it is important to find lenders/equity investors who have experience in loaning and investing in the kind of project you are developing. It is often very helpful to spend time with local bankers who are not necessarily interested in investing in the project but are experienced in real estate transactions. Spending time with banking professionals can be a great trial run for the project concept and to receive constructive feedback on the project plan.

Lawyers: If you want to be a developer, you will need to form a relationship with a real estate *lawyer*. You will find, and have probably already concluded, that most if not all of the steps in the development process involve legal input, negotiation, and review. Try to find a lawyer who has negotiated lease agreements, construction loans, and real estate equity investment agreements, as well as teaming partner contracts. More importantly, find an lawyer that is not only versed in the making of a real estate transaction but also one who is willing to grow with you and can offer appropriate insight and advice. Remember the lender and the equity investors will expect a legal structure and financial approach to their investment that is typical or common in real estate ventures. Having an lawyer versed in the interest of the developer/owner will be important in streamlining negotiations with tenants, lenders, investors, teaming partners, and others and should help limit developer exposure and liability in each step of the process.

Chapter 3: WHO Includes the Project; Tenants, and Users

INTRODUCTION

The ➡ most valuable asset in any real estate development project is the *tenant*. The tenant is the person or entity that will enter into a long-term agreement to pay you rent, bring people to the site, and make it attractive for other businesses and suppliers. The tenant is also typically the reason a buyer might be interested in purchasing the finished project. There are thousands of tenant types, but those with the following credentials will stand out to the debt and equity investors: solid financials, history of successful operations, well-established brand or niche, capable and willing to invest significant cash in *tenant improvement (TI)*, and a financially stable parent corporation as the guarantor. A tenant who brings most if not all of these features to a development is extremely valuable, highly coveted, and sometimes difficult to sign. The reason that tenants that fit this profile can be difficult is that many tenants realize the value they can bring to a development effort and have experience in negotiating these matters. In addition, other developers have probably already identified these valuable tenants and are busy trying to attract them to their development efforts.

The amount of debt and equity you will need to raise can be affected by coveted tenants. If you have one or more of these tenants to anchor the development or even a good mix of smaller tenants with some or all of the above attributes, you are well on the way to attracting the lenders and equity investors needed to get a project financed.

1 TENANT LEASE AGREEMENT

As pointed out, most lenders will require some form of commitment from the potential tenants before they will close on a construction loan. Some lenders for certain property types will accept a *LOI* to lease from the tenants if accompanied by substantial *earnest money* or down payment. The lender will look at this more favorably if the earnest money is "hard," i.e., the potential lessee doesn't get the money back if he decides not to move forward with signing a lease agreement. Generally, however lenders require something more substantial than an LOI to lease with or without earnest money. They want to see a real commitment to lease. This often translates to a full-blown negotiated *lease agreement* that indicates a tenant is legally bound to pay the agreed upon rent and expenses, whether they move in or not! The ➡ lease agreement might be the most important document the developer can produce. It is the document that will be given the most weight by the lenders and equity investors in determining their desire to invest. The lease agreement is so important that in many jurisdictions a memorandum of lease if filed with the deed records at the appropriate county court house to announce to the world that lease rights have been created. The lease agreement becomes the document from which cash flow can be determined, and cash flow typically determines how much a lender will lend and investors will invest. Predictable cash flow also helps determine if the project budget and time line established is a reasonable one for the proposed development. The lease agreement also establishes the ability to meet the debt service coverage or interest coverage ratios discussed in the why and how sections of this book.

2 GETTING THE TENANT TO SIGN A LEASE AGREEMENT

Let us assume that you have a project plan, a site under contract, good teaming partners, and an LOI from a lender and equity investor. Armed with this information, you have been discussing the project with potential tenants. As part of this conversation you disclose to the potential tenant that he will have to sign a legally binding lease agreement (five years or longer). This lease agreement will commit him to pay rent for many years in a building that does not exist yet and probably won't for a couple of years!

As you can probably see this part of the negotiations with the potential tenants can be a challenge. To meet this challenge successfully, the developer needs to educate the tenant on how development projects get completed, how they get financed, and how the tenant fits into the overall picture. Most importantly, however the developer needs to focus on needs and expectations of the tenant and how the project meets or exceeds these needs and expectations.

The first goal is to convince the tenant that the site and project is the best one for thier business. Focus on the combination of all the advantages the project location has to offer to the business and how it solves the tenant's problems! If the tenant is an operator of sports bar and restaurants, you might focus on all parts of the project that will make the venture a success. Traditionally, this will bring the developer to sell all the benefits of the project location. We will discuss what the various benefits of any location might be in more detail when we get to the where chapter of the book. Location is often the single most important feature to a prospective tenant. Once you have the tenant convinced the project and project site meets or exceeds all of his expectations, you can then address the benefits of signing an LOI and more importantly, a binding lease commitment.

By signing the lease agreement the tenants is assured the terms and conditions he wants and needs will locked in and should not change. With the signing of the lease agreement, you will lock in the actual lease space, base lease rate, TI allowance, rent escalation, and all other material terms and conditions. With a signed lease agreement rather than a LOI, you can assure the tenant that no matter what happens to the market place, the basic economic terms are agreed to and will not change. Most new or *green-field* development projects take anywhere from twelve to twenty-four months to complete once financing is closed. It's important for everyone, including the tenant, to know that with the signing a binding lease agreement, they have locked in the terms whether or not the surrounding market rates and terms change.

The signed lease agreement also builds in many safety mechanisms for the tenant. A signed lease agreement will have a construction milestone schedule, agreed upon times of occupancy, initial site, and floor plan for the tenant location, and many other material terms important to the tenant. By signing the lease agreement, both you and the tenant outline all the terms and conditions, so that the project is built and completed on time and as expected.

Finally, you will need to help the potential tenants understand how development projects are financed. They need to understand that lenders and equity investors are putting up millions today for a project that will not generate a return for many years to come. A signed lease agreement with a reputable tenant gives the investors some assurance and a reasonable expectation that the project will be built, and tenants will move in and start paying rent. Of course, don't forget to mention, if applicable, that you are personally guaranteeing the financing of the entire building and that is pretty good insurance to the tenant that you will do all you can to make the project a reality. Discussing the developer guarantee is a good time to bring up the *tenant guarantee*. All lenders and equity providers want some form of tenant guarantee.

3 TENANT LEASE GUARANTEE

It is important that you discuss with the future tenant the need for a guarantee of the lease agreement. Getting the future tenant owners, representatives, or parent company to sign a lease guarantee is another major challenge for the developer. In almost every instance the tenant, tenant owner, or parent company will resist signing or agreeing to sign a guarantee. Much like getting the tenant to sign a lease agreement, getting the owner or parent company of a tenant to sign a guarantee can be a challenge. How to approach this topic with the future tenant will depend on the various circumstances surrounding the tenant and specific project. Since the tenant, parent, or owner is being asked to guarantee performance of the tenant lease, they are agreeing to stand behind the contractual promise of the underlying tenant. They are offering additional assurance that the tenant pay rent, applicable costs, and follow the rules of the building. This is fundamentally a fair request by the developer but not always an easy one to sell to the tenant or tenant parent company or owners. However there is some comfort to the tenant guarantor when you point out that you, the developer, are guaranteeing the entire project investment.

4 THE LETTER OF INTENT: BASIC LOI TERMS

The basic purpose of the tenant LOI is to outline the deal between the developer and the tenants and to outline the basic terms of the lease agreement. The LOI is typically not legally binding but helps give all parties comfort that a deal can be made before substantial time has passed and legal costs are incurred. Here are the basic items you can expect to see in a LOI to lease property in a building that is not yet built.

Basic LOI Terms:

1) The LOI will set forth the tenant entity to be bound by the lease agreement, including the floor or site plan of the space they are leasing and the entity or individuals that will guarantee the lease agreement.

2) *Base lease term and renewal options*, a long initial term or base term for the lease is more attractive to the financing sources and important to the potential buyers down the road. Most tenants will also want multiple options to extend or renew the base term. Tenant renewal options make a lot of sense for the tenant and the landlord developer, but the base lease rate for extension should be at the fair market value rate at time of extension.

3) The base lease rate and how the base lease rate rent increases over the base lease term. The base lease rate is the underlying rental rate the tenants will pay. In addition, the landlord will incorporate annual or regular "bumps" which are increases in the lease rate. Typically these increases will be no less than the increase in the *consumer price index (CPI)* and often scheduled to occur on an annual basis after the first full year. ➡ Rent increases, bumps, or rental escalations are extremely important to you, the lender, equity provider, and potential project buyers down the road. The reason rent escalation is important is that a built-in escalation clause helps keep the base lease rate in check with inflation.

4) Operating expenses and if the cost of the building operations is to be passed through to the tenant. If operating expenses are to be passed through to the tenant, the lease is referred to as *triple net*. The triple net refers to the pass through to the tenant of its proportionate share of the building expenses based on the square footage the tenant is using compared to the total rentable square footage in the building. These triple net or NNN expenses are typically thought of as maintenance, insurance, and taxes. An *absolute triple net lease* or *bond lease* is similar to a triple net lease, but the lease agreement is drafted to take away all legal defenses should the tenant fail to meet their triple net expenses. In a triple net lease the tenant ends up paying these expenses as additional rent each month. Typically, the triple net amount is estimated for the upcoming year and prorated as additional monthly rent. A landlord (developer/owner) may also offer a gross lease. A gross lease does not pass through as additional rent each month the pro rata operating expenses. Typically the landlord utilizing the gross lease has estimated the operating costs and attempted to amortize these into the base lease rate.

5) Once the core and shell of the building are completed, the space must be made suitable for the specific tenant usage. This requires construction of the *tenant improvement or TI*. It is common in most markets for the landlord to pay for some portion of the TI as inducement to a tenant to enter into the lease agreement referred to as the *tenant improve-*

ment allowance. How much TI allowance the developer/landlord might offer to pay is negotiable but is typically driven by the surrounding area market and what other landlords are offering for similar development types. The broker teaming partner will supply this information. It is important to build in the landlord TI allowance into the financial pro forma; more about this later in the outline. It is also important to budget in the pro forma a landlord (developer) management fee for oversight of the TI. It is acceptable in most development projects for the landlord to receive a *management fee* for oversight and coordination of the tenant improvement construction. The fee is typically 3-6 percent of the landlord TI allowance amount (tenants normally resist paying fee on the tenant portion of the TI cost). This provision however is normally inserted in the tenant lease agreement and not commonly found in the LOI.

6) Miscellaneous provisions that are important to consider and sometimes act as inducement to attract key tenants are free rent, usually stated in number of months and often spread out over a couple of years. Landlord developers will often offer free rent and then extend the lease term at the end of the base term to cover the free rent period. For example, if you give six months free rent on a ten-year lease, the base lease term becomes ten years and six months long. Signage can be another key miscellaneous provision important to the tenant. Often the tenant's name on the building can be a key factor for getting a lease commitment. In addition assigned, exclusive, or covered parking, delayed rent payments, and even financing tenant improvement over above the landlord TI allowance can make a difference to potential tenant and give you an advantage over other landlords in the area; more about financing *incremental TI* later in the outline.

Finally, don't forget the real estate brokers representing the transaction. They will require that their representation and fee be set forth in the LOI and of course the developer will rely on the broker for market information related to; rent rates, lease term, escalation clause, TI allowance, free rent, signage, parking, and other tenant benefits and features. Spending time with the real estate broker teaming partner and others that know and work the local market will be the primary source of information necessary to understand how each of these issues should be addressed in the LOI. Of course, you must also make sure that the terms being offered to tenants in the LOI match the financial pro forma that is being used for the project; expect to see considerably more about budgets and pro forma in the why section of the book.

Since tenant interest and, more importantly, tenant commitment is so important to the project, it is important to prioritize this area before approaching the construction lending and equity sources. This translates to spending as much time as possible with those professionals that know and understand the selected market site and product type; in many cases this will help to define the future teaming partners. Often however, the ability to attract tenants to a new development will come back to one fundamental reason: they believe that you and the team you have assembled can deliver the project under the terms and conditions promised.

5 OWNER-OCCUPIED TENANTS

There are certain types of projects that are looked at favorably by commercial construction lenders. One of these types is referred to as *owner occupied*. An owner-occupied real estate development, from the perspective of the construction lender has a couple of advantages. First, they represent a different risk profile for the lender. An owner-occupied facility is historically more stable. The lender will view the company's overall ability to generate profits and its net cash flows to determine its ability to pay rent. Second, banks are heavily regulated and investments in real estate loans cannot typically exceed 300 percent of capital. Under current rules a owner-occupied real estate loan is excluded from this measurement. To be considered owner occupied, the tenant/owner must occupy 51 percent or more of the project. If not, the loan from the banks perspective is classified as an investment in real estate and therefore, included in the 300 percent measurement. The SBA also has certain programs that are oriented favorably toward owner-occupied real estate projects. The SBA programs require the same 51 percent threshold (see the SBA 504 program at www.sba.org).

6 TRENDS IN REAL ESTATE DEVELOPMENT: INTEGRATED PROJECT DELIVERY

As we will discuss in the what section, *design, bid, and build* is the traditional model of how a new construction project approaches the construction phase of development. The architect works with the developer to design the vision. Once the vision is drawn, at least preliminarily, the GC and others are brought in to take the project to the next phase. The design, bid, and build approach requires each potential team member be negotiated with, contracted, and coordinated separately to carry out the project work. This approach and process to a construction project has worked extremely well for many years. However, a recent trend in new project development is referred to as *integrated project delivery (IPD)*. IPD, as the name suggests, is a project delivery approach that brings together all of the disciplines and professionals as part of the same entity, with common goals and incentives. The basic difference between the IPD approach and the *design, bid, and build* approach is with the IPD approach the different team members form a new entity while remaining autonomous professionals. The different teaming partners become invested in the new entity. The new entity enters into a single contract with the developer to design and build the development project with shared corporate governance, common incentives, penalties, and mutually agreed on goals and objectives. From the developer's perspective, utilizing the IPD approach might simplify the development process but this approach is currently the exception and not the normal delivery method.

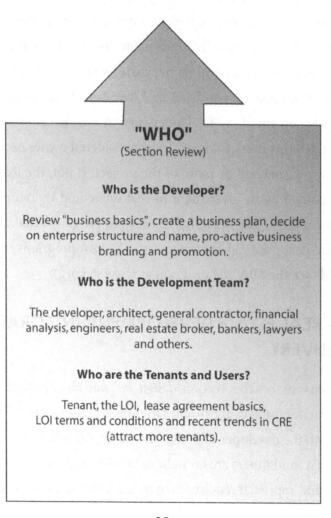

"WHO"
(Section Review)

Who is the Developer?

Review "business basics", create a business plan, decide on enterprise structure and name, pro-active business branding and promotion.

Who is the Development Team?

The developer, architect, general contractor, financial analysis, engineers, real estate broker, bankers, lawyers and others.

Who are the Tenants and Users?

Tenant, the LOI, lease agreement basics, LOI terms and conditions and recent trends in CRE (attract more tenants).

PART 2:
THE WHAT PRINCIPLE

In this section:

What are the basic phases of most, if not all, commercial real estate development projects and what questions must be asked and answered for the specific project being developed?

CHAPTER 4: WHAT ARE YOU GOING TO DEVELOP AND BUILD?

INTRODUCTION: THE GENERAL PHASES OF A TYPICAL COMMERCIAL REAL ESTATE DEVELOPMENT

What are you going to develop and build? Are you developing a retail strip center, multifamily residential building (apartments), medical office building, industrial park, or even a sports bar and restaurant? All of these are unique development property types and have certain specific issues associated with the development effort. Identifying these issues and dealing with them early in the process can and will make a big difference for keeping the vision on track and procuring tenants, debt financing, equity investors, and teaming members.

Before we examine the issues associated with specifically what you want to develop, let's review what the general phases of a typical new commercial real estate development are and the essential components of each phase.

What are the basic phases of most, if not all, commercial real estate development projects? ▪️ This book will address new or *greenbuild* commercial real estate development project in four phases: vision and predevelopment, construction (including TI), management/operations, and sale or refinancing.

Although each phase of a commercial real estate development project is equally important, we will examine most closely the vision and predevelopment effort. We will spend more time focusing on these phases because the developer's primary role is to bring the vision to a concept; the concept to a level others can understand, believe in, and invest in; and to bring the concept and investment to a point where the vision is built. The vision and predevelopment effort requires that the developer be the driving force marshaling all that is necessary to bring the project to a point where tenants commit, construction lenders lend, equity investors invest, city officials approve, and team members devote their valuable time and energy to complete.

There is no construction phase, operations/management phase or sale phase if you don't close the financing. ➡ Therefore, reaching the goal of closing the construction loan is the most important step in the process of the project becoming a reality. Maybe you are now starting to realize the importance of the how in the who, what, where, why, and how principles of commercial real estate development. With the closing of the construction loan (the how), you have made it possible to accomplish the construction of the entire project and three out of the four phases of a typical real estate development project. The only phase left is to refinance or sell the project!

1 VISION AND PREDEVELOPMENT

In order to convert the developer's vision to a project plan, the vision must address, at least generally, the following➡

What are you going to develop and build, where are you planning to build it, and who are you building it for?

With the developer's vision, outlined by the who, what, and where principles, you are able to put together an initial project plan and presentation, and to formulate a budget and financial summary (the why chapter).

With this in mind, listed below is a brief description of many of the key vision and predevelopment issues that a developer needs to simultaneously consider to move the development project forward and to obtain the construction financing.

1 Initial Project and Site Definition: Project vision—what do are you going to develop and build? This requires the following: initial site plans, schematics, renderings and drawings, initial zoning review, environmental/marshlands review, drainage/retention assessment and soils/topography/ trees review, site utilities review, permit and specific regulatory and or surrounding area issues review, and initial assessment.

2 Initial Market Review: Where are you going to build the project? What are the basic demographic characteristics for the market and target niche (generally)? What is the area competition; identify comparable projects and their current status. Make an initial inquiry about market rent rates/tenant improvement allowances/annual rent increases, guarantee expectations, and other market conditions relative to attracting tenants.

3 Initial Tenant Communication: Who are the tenants going to be and how will the project appeal to them? Tenant marketing and presentations should be prepared, site visits made, interest discussions conducted, LOIs drafted, negotiations begun, and lease agreement drafts started. You can spend more time courting and building relationships with tenants and prospective tenants than any other aspect of the predevelopment stage. As noted before, securing rent-paying tenants is the simple most important predevelopment activity. ➠ Tenants represent the key to accessing the Holy Grail of construction financing.

4 Location and Site Due Diligence: Site selection defines location. Once the parcel has been identified, you will need to begin negotiating the purchase contract, earnest money, and ground lease or land transfer agreement. This negotiation will require you to consider and begin researching the following: *purchase price and terms, investigation of property issues, timing, lot size and property lines, earnest money deposit amount, zoning and land use issues, utilities and service, environmental phase I, geological and soils testing, natural hazards, topography, drainage, neighborhood and property conditions, tax issues, tenant-use issues, and who pays for these items.*

5 Initial Project Debt and Equity Presentation: For your initial debt and equity presentations, you will need to prepare a business plan, project executive summary, and initial summary budget/financing analysis/profit analysis. You should also include anticipated tenant mix, commitment levels, and initial market, and target market demographics.

6 Assembly of Teaming Partners: This involves identifying, courting, and selecting the general contractor, architect, engineers, local developers, real estate broker, lawyers, accountants, and others experienced in the development type and project location. You'll need to find a financial analyst partner—the Excel master. You will also need to begin negotiating contract terms and conditions with each of these players.

7 Federal, State, City, County, or Local Authorities: investigation or identification of local, state, county, and federal government issues, including financing, enhancement, incentive and subsidy programs, initial conversations with city and county about entitlement process, permitting, zoning approvals, and special issues associated with the specific parcel and intended use, courting local representatives and dignitaries as appropriate to the project.

Each of the steps mentioned above needs to be considered, analyzed, introduced, negotiated, and moved forward at the same time, so all aspects of the project come together at the right time. We will address each of the above items in detail as we explore the who, what, where, and why sections of the book.

(a) Predevelopment Phase Expenses

In the vision, predevelopment phase of a project the developer is at risk for the expenses incurred. The developer is at risk because until the construction loan closes there is no way to get paid back for project expenses. Many of the teaming partners will risk not getting paid. Most experienced teaming partners know payment for services rendered during the predevelopment stage is dependent on getting the construction loan closed. However, many of the predevelopment service providers, including some of the teaming partners, will expect to be paid when invoiced. Address this issue early in the process with each of the potential teaming partners. Many of CRE professionals are accustomed to working at risk for payment and subject to the construction loan closing. The good news is that if you are successful in closing the construction loan and moving forward with the project, most if not all of these expenses can be budgeted and reimbursed out of the first draw. The bad news is that many of the expenses you incur with teaming partners or others will need to be paid whether or not the project financing is closed and funded. These expenses can vary from a couple of thousand dollars to tens and even hundreds of thousands of dollars, depending on the size and stage of the project.

(b) Transition: Predevelopment to Construction

There comes a time in every project when you have spent so much time and money that it is very difficult and expensive to turn back. That time or dividing line normally comes when it's time to tell the architects to finish the plans and specifications.

Up to this point you have likely spent a considerable amount of money, but the architects plan and specs can run from tens of thousands and even hundreds of thousands of dollars. ➥ The reason there comes a time that the developer must commit to move forward or move on to another project is the requirement of most lenders and even equity investors that the project be *permit ready*. Permit ready means that upon funding or just before funding closes, you can immediately obtain (or pull) the permits needed to begin construction. Every city, county, or municipality typically has some form of permit process that is supposed to be followed, approved, and paid for before a construction project can start. To reach the point where you are ready to pull the permits, you must have brought all the items listed above and more to a point beyond presentations and discussions, and commit to getting them completed. These are expensive but important items! Many lenders will close a construction loan before permits are pulled but will typically not fund until the permits are obtained.

The lender and the equity investor will require that the items listed below be finalized, signed, and in their hands before they fund (see end of the how section for example of equity investor diligence requirements before funding). Here is a list of the most important items you need to commit to and finalize before the equity will invest, and the construction debt can close and fund.

1. *Land Contract.* Secure the site location. You will need to show you have purchased the land parcel or secured the right to purchase the land parcel and are ready to close in sync with the construction loan. To secure the land, you will have paid the landowner *earnest money*. At some point depending on the purchase contract terms this earnest money will go "hard," which is another way of saying you don't get it back. You must either close on the land or lose the earnest money. Moreover it is not uncommon to put up additional earnest money to extend the contract terms.

2. *Environmental Phase I.* No lender or equity provider will invest in today's market without a clean phase I. One of the primary reasons a clean environmental is required is that lenders have been held liable for environmental cleanup issues. This is in large part because of *the Comprehensive Environmental Response, Compensation, and Liability Act* (CERCLA), which is sometimes referred to as the Superfund. *CERCLA* applies a *strict liability* standard related to environmental liabilities. This federal act makes current owners and users

liable for cleanup costs and expenses whether or not they had anything to do with the problem. This strict liability standard has been applied by U.S. courts to lenders, investors, and landowner developers. With this in mind, it is important to the project to get the environmental phase I done early in the process. The phase I is the examination by a qualified commercial entity that the parcel is *free of contaminates* as defined by applicable, federal, state, and local law or regulation. If the phase I identifies an issue, the developer must decide whether to drop the attempt to purchase the selected site or to attempt to *remediate* the problem. Remediation is what that you will need to do if the examiner has found some form of environmental contamination, and you still want to develop the parcel. If remediation is necessary it can be extremely expensive, time consuming, and almost always brings the purchase price of the land back into discussion between the developer and the owner. Earlier in the book we referred to new development projects as greenfield projects. Development projects reclaiming land that is contaminated for new development are often referred to as *brownfield* projects.

3. *Geotechnical Report.* The geotechnical report will help you determine that you can build, what you want to build, and where you want to build based on soils and condition of the land. The soils and conditions can have a serious impact on construction costs. For example if the soils are such that concrete beams or supports drilled deep into the ground are needed to secure the foundation, these supports may add significant unanticipated expense to the development effort.

4. *Engineering Survey.* There are numerous types of surveys required in every development project. The American Land Title Association (ALTA) survey is one of the required surveys. The ALTA survey is a survey to *ALTA standards* that results in a legal description of the property and insured as a survey endorsement on the owner's title policy (see www.alta.org). The other surveys that may be needed include topographic, drainage and retention, land use, tree, and traffic volume. Ultimately, the ALTA title survey is the one that will be attached to the land title policy and relied on by others.

5. *Entitlement, Zoning, and Vested Rights.* Almost every jurisdiction has incorporated some form of *entitlement* process and procedure with which a developer/landowner must comply to move forward with a development project. Entitlement means that

if the developer/landowner meets the established standards they are entitled to have access to public roads, utilities, water, sewer, and other necessities. Assuming of course, these services exist. As part of the entitlement process the developer must also comply with the local zoning regulations. Zoning ordinances and regulations are laws that municipalities and others use to restrict land use to meet local public policy standards. Zoning regulations could prohibit establishment of a sports bar and restaurant next to an established grade school. Early in the development process the developer needs to determine if the land is properly zoned for the intended use. If the land is not properly zoned you can plan to add 3-6 additional months into the overall pre development process. *Vested rights* on the other hand is a *common law* landowner right of defense against overly burdensome zoning restrictions. These two issues, public policy concerns and private property rights, have been at odds since the United States Constitution was ratified, and this conflict is not likely to change any time soon. "Grandfathering" is another important right a developer should explore once the land parcel has been identified or secured. *Grandfathering* is a term used to indicate that the parcel of land in question will not be subject to certain new rules and regulations. The land is grandfathered (previous generation) to the new regulations. This can be important in determining proper zoning, tree ordinances, *impervious to pervious cover* restrictions and other important land use items.

6. *Plat.* The plat is a map of the community, subdivision, or lot. To be valid, a plat must be approved by a local governing authority and legally or properly filed. Once completed, a plat will be assigned *lot and block numbers.* If we were attempting to bring together multiple parcels for our sports bar and restaurant, we might need to *replat* these parcels to match the overall local scheme or plan. We would be required to survey the new lot with the multiple parcels and apply to the local authority to approve the new plat. A new plat or even an amended plat can be both costly and time consuming, adding months to the development process. The plat can be a time consuming and expensive part of the development process and the experienced developer will build in plenty of contingency to extend feasibility or closing if the plat has been delayed at the city approval level.

7. *Will Serve Letters.* Will-serve letters from applicable authorities are letters indicating that basic utilities will and can be supplied to the development site. This would include

water, sewage, telecommunications, and electric. The agreement to supply utilities with the local utility service is referred to as the *utility service agreement* (USA). As part of the USA the municipality will agree to deliver water and sewage. This delivery is often measured in units and referred to as *equivalent dwelling units or EDUs*. Equivalent dwelling units are very important if you are developing heavy users of water and sewage such as multi- family or apartment development efforts. In fact in most jurisdictions the EDU allotment will run with the land and can be conveyed from one buyer to the next.

8. *Architectural Drawings*. These drawings set forth the plans and specifications for the project. The plans and specifications for the project are probably the most important and the most expensive piece of the predevelopment requirements (excluding the cost of the land or site). The plans and specifications are needed not only for the GC and the project budget or schedule of values but to move the project to obtaining permit from local authorities. As we have pointed out earlier, most debt providers will only fund knowing the permit to build has been pulled or will be pulled with the first loan draw and before work begins on the project.

9. *Permitting Process*. Before beginning a building project, whether it is for green build, rehabilitation, renovation, or tenant improvement the developer owner will be required to apply for a permit from the applicable authority. The permitting process can be complicated, time consuming, and expensive; it involves complying with significant regulation, processes, and procedures that often involve simultaneous coordination with numerous regulatory departments and authorities.

10. *Legal*. Almost every facet of the development process involves or should involve legal review. There will be substantial legal fees and time negotiating final documents with landowners (purchase money contracts), tenants (LOI, lease agreement, and guarantees), equity investors (investment documents), debt providers (loan agreements), teaming partners (contracts), and many others.

Just in case you are not convinced that there comes a time when each developer must decide to jump in or stay on the sidelines, consider that the cost associated with the above, which does NOT include the cost of purchasing the land site or earnest money, can easily run into the hundreds of thousands of dollars, depending on the project type and size.

However, if you have done the necessary homework, have committed tenants, brought the debt and equity to a point that they are seriously interested, and have experienced committed teaming partners, you can confidently commit and move forward with all of the above items to close the equity investment and construction loan.

2 CONSTRUCTION PHASE

With the beginning of the construction phase, the vision actually begins to take shape. Permits get pulled, the site gets cleared, leveled, on- and off-site improvements begin or are finished, subcontractors are lined up, foundation or curtain gets laid, equipment is ordered, frame goes up, building envelope begins, electrical and mechanical get dropped, colors get chosen, core and shell forms, a roof gets placed, and the building and surrounding lot generally starts to look like the renderings you have been carrying around and showing to hundreds of people over the past year.

*Table 3: Example of Rendering for a Single Story Office Building
(Tucker, Booker, Donhoff, and Partners Architects)*

(a) The General Contractor and Initial Construction

As we discussed, most construction projects are set up as *design, bid, and build*. Some projects are bid out as *design-build* contracts. Government agencies tend to favor a design build. In a design build, the constructor of the project oversees not only the construction but the design as well.

You may recall that we compared the GC to the quarterback, and that is a perfect description at the construction phase of the development process. Before the involvement of the GC, the developer plays the primary role in coordinating the development, needs of the project, assembling the team, and closing the construction loan and equity investment. However once the loan is closed and funded, for all practical purposes construction becomes the main focus of the project and the GC takes over.

Before the construction loan closing, the GC will do quite a bit of work anticipating the construction start and pulling the permits to build; the GC will review the plans and specs, outline the project construction specifications, generally work with the architects, prepare to pull permits, soft bid the work to suppliers and subs, preliminarily set up and coordinate timing of suppliers and subs, review safety issues, and generally get the project ready to start construction.

Once the loan closes and the construction begins, the developer will be needed for three primary functions related to the construction process: pay application review and draw request; review and approval of change orders; and general oversight of development team, construction progress, and *hand off.*

(b) The Developer Role during Construction

Once the construction phase begins, the developer is regularly involved in the review, approval, and submission of the *application for payment or pay app.* The pay app is a monthly compilation of the bills, invoices, and change orders related to that month's or the previous month's work. Before construction begins and once the construction loan has closed, the developer and the GC will finalize the *schedule of values (SoV).* The schedule of values is is a detailed statement furnished by the contractor outlining the values or portions of each line item that make up the *contract sum.* The contract sum is the GC's total cost estimate to complete the project the GC was contracted to complete. The SoV is used to break out the total contract amount into each of its component parts—item by item. This SoV approach is then used to submit and review progress in the line item each month as the draw for payment is requested. You will recall that construction loans are funded each month based on a request for to draw funds from the construction loan to pay for the work performed. This request for payment is a referred to as the draw. The SoV will usually consist of a description of the work, the values (cost) associated with the completed work, and the remaining balance needed to finish the work. Think of it as a very complete and detailed rolling budget that allows you to view the entire budget, the immediate request for funding (the draw), expenditures to date on each line item, and what is left in the budget to spend on each line item.

To create the SoV, the GC will determine the core and shell values or the *hard-cost estimates*. Hard costs are costs specifically associated with the construction of the *core and shell and site costs*, and preparing and surrounding the construction site. *Soft costs* are costs not specifically associated with hard construction and include architectural and developer fees. The total of hard and soft costs makes up the project budget. The GC should submit to the developer each month the hard cost payment request in the form of a SoV. The developer is expected to take this information on the hard cost, add the soft cost and all other cost items, and submit the proposed monthly pay app request to the bank to approve a draw of the funds from the construction loan. The developer can often work in concert with the GC to produce a single monthly pay application, containing all costs to submit to the construction lender.

As pointed out, once the monthly pay app is completed and reviewed, the developer is responsible for signing and submitting the monthly draw request to the construction lender for funding. The construction lender will not only review the request internally but will often have hired a third party *construction manager or CM* to review as well. The CM is often utilized by construction lenders to oversee construction projects. The CM's role can range from daily oversight of the construction process, to merely reviewing the draw request and work performed monthly.

The project lender and equity provider will want regular updates during the construction phase, and they are typically most focused on whether the project is on budget and on schedule. The lender will also want to know that no liens or encumbrances have been placed on the property. In most states *contractors, including subcontractors,* have a *statutory lien* on the work they perform for a construction project. Getting a release of this lien before each month's payments insures the developer and the bank that the subcontractors and suppliers were paid and that the project remains lien free. The contractor should require the subcontractors sign a *release of lien* form upon receipt of payment each month and a completion affidavit when applicable. This *release of lien* form should then be included with each monthly pay application request from the GC. If a subcontractor files a lien, and the lien is disputed, a developer or the GC can *bond around* a lien claim. Bonding around the lien claim effectively removes the lien from the title by indemnifying any buyer or lender.

Another issue to consider is that a part of each monthly pay application is the *hold back or retention.* Although the monthly draw will invoice the full amount owed to the contractor and subcontractors typically, 10 percent of the monthly invoiced amount is held back or retained as additional security that the work was and/or is being performed. In many states the contract retention amount is determined by statute. At the end of the construction process the retention becomes payable. This is important for the developer to understand because the retained payment amount is often viewed as incentive for the GC and subcontractors to stay focused on the project through completion. However, as the project core and shell starts to appear completed, the subcontractors will start to get concerned about their retention amounts being paid. Some will even file liens before the developer has a chance to review the issues and approve payment of the retention. In any event, as the building begins to look like a completed project, the developer needs to become more involved, and retention payment is one area of focus.

During the course of construction numerous issues will arise that relate to changes, modifications, improvements, or unaddressed issues in the architects plans and specs. These changes and issues can become *change order* requests. Change orders probably create more issues for the developer than any other items that arise during construction. As these issues come to the surface, the GC will request that the developer make a change to the original plans. The GC should outline in writing what the issues are, why they arose, what is the proposed solution, the incremental cost or savings to the project, and how he proposes or recommends the new or modified work be applied to the budget and SoV. The developer will be required to sign off and approve the various change orders before they become final. Change orders can represent a difficult area for the developer. You may not be versed in the issues associated with and related to the requested change order. If you have engaged a CM or the lender or equity provider has engaged a CM, it can be helpful to ask him to review change order requests.

During construction the GC will organize regular construction progress meetings to update project status, follow up on issues from previous meetings, review change orders, and discuss new issues that have arisen. If for some reason the GC is not organizing regular progress meetings, the developer should. These regular meetings keep you abreast of what is going on with the project, project schedule, the budget, and the monthly draw; they also help keep you in touch with the GC and the various players involved in the construction process. Historically, most of the problems that arise in a development project arise or surround the monthly payment process and work performed during construction. Since the developer must sign off on all pay apps and draws, approve change orders, and regularly report to the debt provider and equity investor, staying involved on a regular basis during construction is extremely important.

As the construction nears completion, the building starts to move toward the management/operations phase, the hand-off from the GC back to the developer begins. One major hand-off issue that involves the contractor and the developer for both the core and shell, and TI construction is the *punch list or to-do list*. A punch list is actually a part of the original contract document with the contractor and should be completed before the contractor is paid in full, and the retention is released. The punch list is triggered when the contractor informs the developer the project is substantially complete. The GC should also give to the developer a final building inspection and certificate of occupancy from the appropriate city agency. Once the contractor has declared the project to be substantially complete and delivers the *certificate of substantial completion,* the developer should organize a walk through, during which a punch list is created. The punch list is the owner's and lender's chance to make sure they got what they paid for and should be completed before retained payment is released. Typically, the developer will have the architect of record help create the punch list and then verify performance and completion of the work. Once the work associated with the punch list is completed, a final report is issued, punch list signed off on, and retention or final payment can be released to the GC and others.

One final note related to the GC hand off of the completed core and shell. The GC should organize and supply a *warranty, maintenance, and service manual binder* that contains all agreements, warranties, manuals, and other related information to the building's many different mechanical, electrical, and plumbing functions. In addition the developer should organize meetings between the building manager and GC. These meetings are important to ensure that the basic processes and procedures related to the building are agreed to and understood. In addition it is a good idea to have the GC put together contact information for all the subcontractors and suppliers who worked on the project. Sooner or later the developer or building management will want to contact one or more of the subcontractors or suppliers for issues that arise well after construction completion.

(c) Tenant, Build Out, and Construction

There comes a time in every new CRE development effort where the building or buildings seem complete. The walls, roof, interiors, utilities, and parking have all come together, and the building looks finished, except there is one thing, one very important thing, missing—tenants. At this stage of the construction the building is often referred to a *warm or vanilla shell*. A warm shell can have HVAC (heating, ventilation, and air conditioning), bathrooms, elevator, and even drop ceiling and slab but does not have the necessary construction to get the tenants moved into the building. A *cold white box* is a building with minimal interior finish out which may include ceilings, lighting, plumbing, interior walls, elevators, rest rooms, and a concrete floor. It is essentially same as a vanilla shell or warm shell building, but without a heating and cooling system. A *cold shell* is a building core and shell without most if not all of the additions mentioned above. Getting the specific space for the tenants agreed to, designed, permitted, contracted for, and built is commonly referred to as the tenant's *space plan or floor plan* and often referred to as *tenant improvement or TI*.

During the construction of the core and shell, the developer should also focus on the tenant and tenant construction. Each tenant space must be designed, reviewed, and approved to adapt the lease space for the operating business. Many tenants will have an architect from a previous project and previously approved basic floor plan design they want to utilize. However the space plan must be adapted to fit and work with the leased space in the new building. Therefore the tenant architect and tenant TI contractor will have to coordinate and work with the project architect and possibly the project GC to discuss and understand specific issues between the existing structure and the tenant space plan and design.

Completing the tenant space plan can be a difficult and lengthy process. There may be a new architect and contractor, and tenants often involve numerous personnel inside their organization in the process of determining how the space should be finished. Final tenant sign off can take months, and you will need to have the space plan and design before you can complete the permitting process. In most jurisdictions, there is a separate permitting process for the tenant build-out construction, and this process can add months to the construction phase.

When the tenant engages a different architect and or contractor to do the TI, just the coordination between these different groups can be a challenge. The developer does have important input as to the tenant TI build out because he has likely given the tenant a *TI* or *build out allowance*. As we discussed earlier in the book TI allowance is the amount of tenant improvement the developer/landlord is willing to pay to entice the tenant to the project. In addition the tenant's TI process and procedures are almost always addressed in the lease agreement. The lease agreement will typically address the treatment of the developer/landlord TI allowance but also how to bid and construct the actual tenant TI. The lease agreement should also address the developer/landlord construction management fee for the oversight of the TI improvements. This provision is typically found in an addendum to the lease agreement and not the LOI. As the developer do not overlook the importance of being involved during the TI build out and installation. The tenant is the customer of the developer and not of the contractor or architect. If there are complications or complaints the tenant will look to the developer to resolve.

(d) Competitively Bidding out Tenant Improvement

Often the tenant will want the developer/landlord to bid out the construction work for the TI. If the tenant wants the developer to help competitively bid out the tenant TI work, the developer will need to work closely with the team architect to address the following tasks. First, the team architect should write a specification for the build-out project. In addition to *material and scope* specifications, the architect will need to add front-end specifications that state general requirements and expected contractual obligations. Finally, working with the tenant, you need to establish the interior finishes for the project, supply the architect with a list of bidders, a bid date, where bids are to be received, and a way to fairly and equitably answer bidder question. Answers to questions from bidders should be supplied at the same time to all parties with sufficient time before the bid date to allow incorporation into each bid. Answers to questions on a piecemeal basis from other bidders can create problems from other bidders, and you may not end up with an apples-to-apples comparison at bid date.

This bid process is similar to what the GC should do in selecting the appropriate subcontractors and suppliers when they are establishing a hard costs bid on the product or service for the final project budget and SoV.

The developer and team architect can also utilize this process or a similar process and procedure if the plan is to bid out the general contractor role for the construction of the core, shell, and surrounding improvements.

Finally, don't forget about the construction lender and equity providers. With the core and shell close to completion, they have probably already started to focus on the project budget and financial projections. The financial projections would have outlined a clear path to when rent would begin. Rent, as we have discussed, gives the project cash flow, and cash flow allows expenses to be paid, including the interest payments on the construction loan. Of course, getting the tenant improvements completed and tenants moved in is the best way to get them to begin paying rent!

With tenants moving in, the project begins to take on a new life. It begins to operate and function like an operating facility, serving tenants, customers, and the public.

3 MANAGEMENT AND OPERATING PHASE

A couple of months before completion of the core and shell but well before the final building inspection and tenant improvement starts, the hand off begins. The hand off is the point in time when the GC has completed or is about to complete all the things he was contracted to do and now gives the completed core and shell product back to the developer/landlord.

How the building will be managed and operated after completion is usually an important discussion point between the developer and the equity provider, and usually occurs at the time the development agreement is negotiated. There are a couple of very good reasons for this. First, a professionally managed building is important for attracting and retaining tenants. Second, there is a lot of work associated with managing a commercial real estate operation, and the lenders and equity investors who have a lot at stake want to assure the building(s) are properly managed. The following is just a short list of some of the functions a management company needs to perform as the hand off between the constructor and management begins:

> manage tenant improvement • facilitate tenants moving in • review and understand lease agreements • collect deposits and initial rents • coordinate utilities • ensure functioning of telecommunications,• establish safety reporting for fire alarm and elevator • ensure building security functioning • handle HVAC and equipment maintenance schedules, service agreements, and initial warranty compliance • initial budget reporting

There is another good reason for using an experienced professional third party management group—the sale of the building or project. Most institutional buyers prefer the building be professionally managed even if most buyers plan to insert their own management. A professional third-party management company gives potential buyers some comfort that the building is being properly managed and operated. The lender, equity provider, tenants, developer/landlord, and potential future buyers all expect a well-run building. Hiring a professional management company creates a comfort level that things will get done efficiently and appropriately.

(a) Developer Managed and Operated Buildings

Many developers prefer to manage the project property themselves. This approach can work well, but you need to address this desire early in discussions with the debt and equity. The debt provider and equity investors will need to be convinced you have the experience and capabilities to manage a functioning CRE project. There is a lot to do in professionally managing a commercial real estate development that is open and full of tenants. Below is a list of some of the general property management duties an operator manager of a typical CRE building should expect to oversee, manage, and perform:

> tenant services (as defined in the lease and building rules and regulations) • tenant retention program • property maintenance • building supplies • property

inspections • service contracts • rent collections • delinquency notices • tenant rent escalations and reconciliations • tenant TI and move ins • tenant move outs • budget and financial reporting • collection of insurance certificates • handling emergency situations • oversight of management policies and guidelines • accounting responsibilities • construction management supervision as needed or requested • operating reports as requested • additional services as defined by the landlord/developer/owner and tenants.

As this list shows, there is a lot to do in managing and operating a successful commercial real estate development. As compensation for all of the work involved, building managers are typically paid between 3-6 percent of collected rent, depending on the market location, property type, and tenant mix.

4 SALE OR REFINANCE PHASE

What started with a vision and project plan grew into a viable concept depicted by the architect, took the shape of a building with the leadership of the general contractor, was fully leased with tenants by you and the real estate broker, transformed into an efficient operating entity by management, and is now a complex working operation. The project is *stabilizing*. A stabilized building can be defined as a building that is basically full of rent-paying tenants, and the management company is handling most the development operations. Stabilized also means you have enough net cash flow that you can meet the day-to-day expenses and service the interest on the construction loan. With a stabilized building, we move to the next step in the development process—the sale or refinancing phase.

(a) Why Buy a Stabilized Building

Why would someone want to buy an existing building that is rented by others? What would make this purchase a good investment? There are not that many components to consider in making this determination, but it's not always easy to do successfully.

When a building is purchased ➡ the buyer trades cash now for the right to receive rent each year minus out-of-pocket costs over the time estimated they would own the building. A purchaser is also hoping to get something for the building when it's sold in the future (referred to as *reversion*) and probably wants to make a profit. That's pretty much it. Invest now, collect rent, pay expenses, and sell for profit. When you take all these components, throw them into a formula, and add a *yield* you can determine the return a purchaser can reasonably expect. With this calculation, you can begin to understand why someone would buy a stabilized building.

(b) Selling the Project

In the how section, we discussed how a construction loan is typically short term. At the end of the loan term, it must be refinanced to a more permanent loan type or miniperm. A miniperm is short term financing used to pay off the construction loan. In the equity chapter of the same section, we addressed that the equity investor was or would be focused on how long his money would be tied up before he could exit and realize a return on his investment. Together you, the team financial analyst, the debt provider, and the equity investor modeled in the *profit analysis* a reasonable period of for construction and stabilization of the project, and therefore a possible sale or refinancing. Hopefully the crystal ball used a year or two ago to make the projection for the project was right, and the building stabilized well before or just in time to refinance the project.

The process of looking to sell or refinance a project will start to take shape long before the project is stabilized. In fact, you should be talking and working with potential buyers throughout each of the project's four development phases. In the predevelopment phase, you put together a *project plan, project budget, financial analysis, and profit analysis*. Part of this process required research of historical *cap rates* for comparable properties and other purchase factors such as cost of sale. Cap rates for comparable properties are important because they shape the actual selling price you might receive for the project. We will examine in some detail the financial analysis and cap rate application in the why section of the book.

Chapter 5: What Are the Specific Issues Related to the Product Type and Location?

Now that we have reviewed the four phases of a typical new build or greenfield commercial real estate development project, we need to examine what issues must be considered and what questions asked and answered for the specific project to be developed.

What you specifically plan to develop coupled with the location and the users will identify numerous specific issues you will need to address early in the predevelopment phase. There are so many issues that evolve around location, product type, and the tenant users that it is best to start with a competent professional to help identify and resolve all the issues associated with the specific development. For example, a medical complex will often require greater parking requirements, as well as specific parking challenges like increased handicapped spaces and ambulance ingress and egress. Thus a medical development may require a larger site than you originally anticipated. In addition to unique parking issues, medical facilities often have noise restrictions, oxygen and special gas services, backup generator needs, increased fire protection, and special licensing requirements. Using the sports bar and restaurant example, many jurisdictions do not allow alcohol to be served in an establishment located within a certain distance of a school or church. Identifying and attempting to resolve these specific issues early in the development effort is where the team architect and local engineering pool are invaluable. However as the developer, you should gain a little insight into some of the issues before the project starts, and you incur substantial cost and expense. You can get a head start on many of these issues by visiting with the city's planning and development office and/or Web site.

1 PREDEVELOPMENT: CITY PLANNING AND LAND DEVELOPMENT OFFICE

Most city planning and development offices are extremely helpful in guiding developers through the local development process for a CRE project. Most cities today (even the smaller ones) not only have a specific office dedicated to assisting developers but also may have a Web site specifically designed to help developers through the cumbersome process of obtaining the building permit and analyzing the multitude of issues that need to be considered to be confident the project can be built as planned. Many cities present these issues in a step-by-step format making it easy for the new developer to get a good summary of the process and procedures.

2 PROPERTY ACQUISITIONS: CONTRACT TO PURCHASE LAND

Let us assume you have the ideal site picked out for the sports bar and restaurant, and you have lined up a tenant restaurant operator that likes the site. With this in mind, you must then acquire the site or at least secure the rights to develop the site. There are multiple ways to acquire the site or property: you can enter into an agreement to purchase the land, ground lease the land, or even partner with the landowner to acquire the land. A *ground lease* is the long-term right to develop improvements on the land usually for a period of twenty years or more. In a ground lease, title to the underlying property is not transferred, but the right to develop improvement on the land is transferred by a long-term lease. Most lenders and equity investors are quite familiar with the ground lease as a form of ownership. For example, medical office buildings on a hospital campus are very often ground leased to the developer for the purpose of building the medical office buildings with landownership maintained by the hospital group. To satisfy the first-lien needs of the lender, the owner of the site (the *ground lessor*) will subordinate the improvement to the construction loan lender but will keep a ownership of the underlying land.

It is also common to discuss with the landowner the possibility of using the land as equity and having the landowner join the partnership group developing the project. Many landowners often look for developers that can bring product niche expertise, knowledge of the community, and experience associated with what a landowner might consider the *highest and best use,* for the land.

Although the ground Lease and partnering with the landowner may be two potential options to acquire the right to develop the land, most developers want to acquire a piece of property *fee simple,* which means the developer will acquire full and unrestricted title to the land (subject only to the title policy exceptions).

How do you acquire a parcel or the right to own or develop a parcel or site? First, you typically negotiate an *earnest money contract or contract to purchase land* (EMC). An earnest money or contract to purchase land should give you the right but not the obligation to purchase the site. Working with the landowner and/or his broker, you will normally negotiate a price and other important terms. You will put earnest money down to hold the land while you conduct due diligence. The diligence period is often referred to as the *feasibility or contingency period*. Due diligence is extremely important in helping you determine whether or not this site will work for the project type and user. ➡ Due diligence gives the buyer an opportunity to conduct an inspection and determine if what you want to build can be built on the site, as well as help you analyze what issues, if any, might prevent, delay, or cost you money in developing the site.

Here is a short list and brief summary of some of the items typically addressed in a EMC that need to be reviewed, understood, and agreed to as you consider signing the EMC, and move closer to purchasing the land and starting the development project. Your team's real estate broker will be instrumental in helping negotiate the EMC and incorporate the local norms for the many different issues specifically related to the project use and location.

Earnest Money Contract or Contract to Purchase Land: Typical Questions to Ask and Answer

Property Location and Description

Proposed Purchase Price

Earnest Money Deposit: amount, time frame secured by payment, additional deposit for extension of time, forfeiture, and terms if you don't purchase.

Finance Terms: seller financing terms, if any, assumable financing, or subject to buyer obtaining financing contingency and financing timing.

Closing contingencies: timing of removal of contingency items such as receipt of acceptable valuation and or appraisal and/or financing.

Due Diligence: feasibility or contingency period, time frame and extensions.

Dispute Resolution process and procedure.

Cost of due diligence and allocation to buyer and seller: inspections, title policy, survey, and appraisal, and who pays for what services during the due diligence period. The real estate broker teaming partner will know how costs are typically allocated between buyer and seller.

Disclosures: seller disclosures such as easements, leases, restrictions, environmental, and other conditions affecting property.

Buyer's investigation of property (the due diligence): investigation of lot size and property line, entitlement, zoning and land use, utilities and service agreements, environmental hazards, geological and soils, natural hazards, neighborhood, and property conditions, historical issues, tax issues (roll back), rental property issues, site ingress and egress, and tenant issues. Roll back taxes are indication of prior agricultural use and many jurisdictions will "roll back" applicable tax status to the new use to capture tax revenue triggered by the transaction and new use.

Title company: land title policy and exceptions.

Escrow (monetary deposit): escrow instructions.

Brokers: buyer and seller broker identified and how they are to be paid.

Conditions to close: tenant signing lease agreement, closing of needed financing, clear title, appraisal, and lot acceptable for intended us.

These are just a short list of issues normally addressed in the EMC. Of course, entering into the earnest money contract or contract to purchase land is just the start of pursuing the actual purchase of the property. As you can see from the list above, you must conduct, complete, and pay for the due diligence on all of the issues mentioned to ensure there aren't any substantial surprises that would prevent or delay building the intended project.

3 PURCHASING THE LAND VERSUS FINANCING THE PROJECT

Acquiring the land or site does not mean the project will attract financing. If the intention is to begin developing with the acquisition of the parcel, you must move the many other vision/predevelopment phase issues along simultaneously with the due diligence associated with the possible purchase of the land. ➡ Ask yourself if you want to own this land if you can't develop the project? If the answer is no, then before you purchase the land, the developer (you) must be in a position to finance the entire project. This typically means there are signed tenant lease agreements, enough equity to interest a lender, or a guaranteed takeout of the construction loan, and you are satisfied that the major *what* issues will not prevent the planned project development.

This concept of having to ask and answer most of the important questions outlined in the predevelopment phase as well as conducting the due diligence necessary to be comfortable closing the land purchase (fortunately many of these issues overlap) will also lead you to negotiate the longest due diligence time period possible. You will almost certainly need a longer feasibility period than you think to accomplish and complete the diligence on the land purchase especially when you couple this land due diligence with the work associated with the overall project financing. To make matters more difficult the land seller will want to keep the feasibility time period as short as possible. Be prepared to put up additional cash or *earnest money* for any extensions of time of the contingency period. More money, more time, and more opportunity to address all the important issues related to the project, not just the important issue of purchasing the land.

Of course, with the purchase of the land you have determined location. As we have discussed, location is often considered the single most important factor associated with the success of a commercial real estate project. ➡ Why is location so important? Location attracts tenants and tenants pay rent and rent paying tenants attract the financing needed to build the development effort. The three keys to developing a commercial real estate project are; location, tenants and financing.

If you have been paying attention to the principles set forth in this outline you probably now understand the importance of financing. The where section will examine many of the reasons the real estate mantra of location, location, location is so important.

4 TRENDS IN REAL ESTATE DEVELOPMENT: GREEN BUILDING, LEED CERTIFICATION, AND SUSTAINABILITY

Sustainable development or green building has become a very important trend in real estate development over the last twenty years. The basic premise of green building is energy efficiency. The stated goal of sustainable or green building development is to construct and design buildings in such a way that occupancy and operations result in *zero energy consumption*. In the United States and a limited number of other countries, *LEED certification* has become the standard for green status. Green status is awarded by certification under the LEED credit system, a participatory point program that was designed and is administered by the *U.S. Green Building Council* (see www.usgbc.org).

The LEED system has four levels of achievement for new construction—certified, silver, gold, and platinum. A new development project is awarded credits or points for certain green design categories. These are water efficiency, indoor environmental quality, *sustainability,* energy and atmosphere, materials, and resources. As you add credits for meeting the requirements set up in these five basic areas, you move up the spectrum of green certification. The U.S. Green Building Web site can guide the developer and development team on the specifics.

The largest obstacle in today's world to designing and constructing green is the perceived additional cost. Sustainability comes at a price. The developer must justify the additional up-front cost to the project budget with arguments that it will result in future operational efficiencies. More importantly the developer may be able to show increased tenant flow and interest because of the green or LEED status. However regardless of cost to the project and perceived effect on project margins, LEED certification is becoming more and more prevalent in new construction and major renovations. Many jurisdictions are beginning to adopt and incorporate green, sustainability standards into permitting process and approvals. Green is quickly becoming the legal and moral standard for construction of new development projects.

There is also a LEED accreditation for real estate professionals, contractors, architects, engineers, designers, and others. Real estate professionals that achieve LEED status can add this to their credentials and present themselves as LEED certified. LEED certification is becoming increasingly prevalent among new development projects, and real estate professionals and jurisdictions are incorporating green requirements into development permit requirements. Developers should expect LEED certification, green building, and sustainability to become a required development and construction standard, and begin incorporating these features and processes into future development projects.

"WHAT"
(Section Review)

What are the Four Basic Phases of every CRE
Development Project

Vision and Pre Development

What are you going to build, where are you going to build it
and who are you building it for and the issues related to
transitioning from pre-development to construction.

Construction

On and off site improvement, core and shell construction,
tenant improvement or build out and the developers role
during construction.

Management and Operations

Sale or Refinancing

What are the specific issues related to the project yype and
location?

Contract to purchase land, earnest money and general
terms and conditions. Green development and LEED
certification

PART 3:
THE WHERE PRINCIPLE

In this section:

The where principle focuses on location and the demographics of the surrounding general market, target market, analysis of the proposed specific use, and therefore, why the project location makes sense.

Chapter 6: Where is the Project Located?

INTRODUCTION

As discussed earlier in this outline, the generally accepted mantra for putting a real estate development project on a successful track is *location, location, location.* Pick up any article about real estate, look at any Web site, or watch any show on television today and you'll find that most real estate decisions are based on location. It may be the single most important factor for attracting and retaining tenants, especially those desirable financially stable tenants. Location, as we demonstrated in the what section, is relevant to what you are planning to develop and for whom you are developing it. You wouldn't want to put an industrial development next to a subdivision or a restaurant and bar next to a church. Of course, we now know, based on the what section that you probably couldn't do it anyway. There are many aspects associated with a specific location that are relevant to why the land parcel is the right location for a project. We have already covered some of these factors, including code restrictions, zoning, permitting, ordinances, historical settings, or practical restrictions like acreage. A multifamily apartment site for example will typically need more acreage than a bank site and as mentioned previously, a sports bar and restaurant typically cannot be built close to a school or church.

The where section is made up of a detailed analysis of the *market* that surrounds, encompasses, and makes up the development area and how these relate to the product type. Where helps you zero in on the use, the users, and why the location makes sense.

The market analysis for the purpose of determining whether or not a location is a good one for the project can be broken down into three general areas of review: general area analysis, target area analysis, and specific use analysis.

1 GENERAL AREA ANALYSIS

Each project is designed and built with the idea of attracting certain tenants, users, and customers. The general area analysis is a look at all aspects of the area in the general location of the development site; it helps the developer to better understand who the tenants, users, and customers might be at that location. If you were developing a project in San Antonio, Texas, you would likely consider San Antonio or south Texas as the general area. The debt and the equity for the project will want to analyze what kind of market San Antonio/south Texas might be. Is San Antonio a growth market with more people moving in than out? Is it attracting the growing segments of the marketplace— retirees or baby boomers? If more people are moving in or the population is stable you will want to know why. Does the local economy have a strong employment base, good industry stakeholders, prospects for growth, low unemployment, cooperative city and state government, low taxes, and development incentives? What characteristics might be unique or important to San Antonio that will continue to contribute to the positive growth of the general market? The analysis of the general area will lead you to examine the *demographics* for the area. Demographics for the general market analysis will typically take a look at population make up, size, growth rates, and other market area factors. To follow through with our example, in 2007 the U.S. Census Bureau ranked San Antonio as the ninth largest and fastest growing city in the United States with a growth rate of 5.9 percent per year. The unemployment rate is low and the military, health care, and tourism industries play a major part in the economy's success. The Hispanic population is strong, stable, and growing. Studies have shown baby boomers like the warm climate and low cost of living index found in south Texas. All of these market demographic factors add up to a plus for San Antonio, Texas!

2 TARGET AREA ANALYSES

The target area analysis consists of those characteristics of the market that are specifically associated with the intended use and the specific neighborhood surrounding the project site. If you were developing a hospital in San Antonio, health care would generally be considered the target niche. With this in mind, you would want to do a very detailed study of the health care market in San Antonio. Is health care an important industry that appears to be growing and an integral part of the city's success? If so, understanding the reasons why will be important to helping others such as the debt provider, equity investors, and teaming partners to understand that it makes sense to invest in a health care project in San Antonio, Texas.

Since we are assuming you have answered all aspects of the developer's vision, we can assume that you know what you want to build, where you want to build it, and who you want to build it for. Since you have chosen a location you will want to analyze the neighborhood surrounding the location. If you want to build a hospital in the northwest section of San Antonio, you would analyze the surrounding population, the demand for health care services, and the population demographics of those patients and others currently utilizing the hospitals in the target area's niche market. This would lead you to analyze the market demographics of the actual and surrounding area of the proposed hospital. Questions to answer would include: where do the patients come from and why, what health care services are they generally seeking, and how does this relate to the project location and use?

As you might have already guessed, it doesn't take long for the equity investor or the lender to enter the picture. In almost every instance debt or equity will require a market study prepared by an independent third party that will define the overall general market, demographics, specific or targeted area niche, comparable projects, and outline of the general and specific competition associated with the targeted market niche. The market study would consider any submarkets that appear important to the overall assessment and analysis of the project. Finally, keep in mind that the developer gets to pay for any third-party market study, so the more market data you have to start with, the better.

3 SPECIFIC USE ANALYSES

If the submarket or target market makes sense for the new hospital, you would need to take a hard look at any entity comparable to the intended use that currently exists. This is where the specific use analysis is valuable. In the hospital example, the developer would be expected to do a complete assessment of the relevant *competition* for comparable hospitals within a reasonable distance from the project. This would include specific market, target market, general market, and even national market information. A competitive analysis will reveal projects in the area that are appealing to the customers/users your project hopes to attract. The study should include details on how many competing projects there are and where they are located, the specifics of why they are comparable, and basic data associated with the success or failure of the comparable entities. The specific market analysis will also drill down to issues that are important for attracting tenants. Issues like base rent rates, TI allowance, free rent allocations, NNN charges, tenant make up, vacancy percentages, and other specific but important factors. All this information is valuable and will be needed to put together the project plan and financial analysis. The specific information related to comparable competitive projects in the specific and surrounding area must be analyzed to accurately determine the development project's chance for success.

Finally, the analysis of the comparable competition in the specific market along with the target and general market data needs to be compared to the proposed project and should ultimately lead to justification that there is a clear need for the intended project.

4 DEMOGRAPHIC RESEARCH

You know what you want to build, where you want to build it, and who you want to build it for. Now you need to do the demographic research to support the basic premise that the project makes sense. How do you find the demographic data and more importantly how do you find reliable, current, and relevant data?

The Internet is a great place to begin your research, especially at the vision and predevelopment stage of the project. With a few Internet searches, you can locate commercial real estate Web sites devoted to reporting general-market, target-market, and specific-use data for most jurisdictions and cities. However the Internet will not be reliable for all the project's informational needs. While the Internet can give instant access to worldwide data, you must find timely, relevant local data that reflects the most recent transactions and information. The Internet might be very helpful in finding data related to the general market area and basic data related to the target market and specific use, however information concerning the target market and specific use issues is often more difficult to address if the Internet is your sole source. There are other sources that can give you the information you need to complement what the Internet provides.

First and foremost, don't forget the real estate broker teaming partner. The real estate broker for the project should be the single most valuable source of current, local information. If you've chosen wisely, the real estate broker can offer the best data and insight into the general market, target market, specific-use market, as well as the competition and comparables of the chosen location and use. The real estate broker should know the most recent comparable sales, lease transactions, and pending transactions in the area surrounding the target market niche and site, and should also know the specific information associated with each. If he does not, he will have the ability to gather the information once you discuss with the project. The real estate broker will have access to numerous sources of information including the *multiple listing service* (*MLS*), which is the realtors' proprietary information and like the Internet, a good source for important data.

5 SOURCES OF INFORMATION

Courthouses are often great sources for specific information. Certain states require that specific information be disclosed with the filing of the deed of ownership transfer. Find out if the state in which the project land is located is a *non-disclosing* or *disclosing state*, and you can discover significant information about the comparable projects that have traded or sold. A common published source for information is the local business journal or newspaper. Most jurisdictions have a business journal that is known in the community to follow real estate transactions in the area. Another good source for information can be the property seller. Most sellers have spent some time gathering information that tends to put the property for sale in the best light. Ask if there has been an appraisal on the property, and if so, get a copy of the report. An appraisal will ask and answer most of the questions needed to be addressed and updating the data is easier than creating the data. However the most accurate way to gather the needed data is to dig into the area where you want to build and get the information firsthand. This requires speaking to other real estate brokers, bankers, landowners, current tenants, and attending groundbreaking ceremonies, open houses, and receptions. Don't hesitate to call the surrounding area buildings to ask the landlords or agents about leasing information. Staying active in the local market and with current and prospective users in the area is a great way to stay on top of transactions that are relevant to the project you are promoting. Finally, there are numerous real estate oriented services available on the Internet that will provide information for a fee. These services can be invaluable to help determine basic demographics and local market data. The downside is the ability to determine whether the information is complete.

Do not forget the debt provider and the equity investor will likely want an independent third-party market study to be performed to validate the data you present and to give them assurance that the data is reliable and complete. Producing this data in the project plan and then having it validated by a third-party market study will go a long way in helping you gain the confidence of the investors. The information gathered is also essential for the formulation of the financing analysis and profit analysis. Much of the key information needed to determine the financial viability of the project will be based on the data you gather related to location. There will be more about the financing and profit analysis in the *why* chapter.

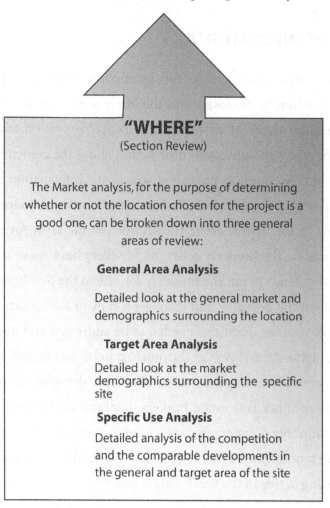

"WHERE"
(Section Review)

The Market analysis, for the purpose of determining whether or not the location chosen for the project is a good one, can be broken down into three general areas of review:

General Area Analysis

Detailed look at the general market and demographics surrounding the location

Target Area Analysis

Detailed look at the market demographics surrounding the specific site

Specific Use Analysis

Detailed analysis of the competition and the comparable developments in the general and target area of the site

PART 4:
THE WHY PRINCIPLE
WHY IS THE PROJECT
GOING TO SUCCEED?

In this section:

Why is a unique mix of the developer's vision and the who, what, and where, principles of commercial real estate development. When we get to why, we must demonstrate to the construction lender, equity investors, tenants, teaming partners, community leaders, and others that this project makes good sense and is worthy of their time, money, and effort.

INTRODUCTION

What is the perspective of the lender or equity investor when looking at the potential project investment? They have a limited amount of money to invest, multiple opportunities to invest, and a defined time frame in which to realize a return on their investment. Therefore, most lenders or investors want to invest in projects that involve an experienced developer and development team and a project type they know and have had success with in the past. They are most interested in projects proposed for an attractive high-growth location and that have significant tenant leasing commitments, parent company guarantees, and plenty of potential interested buyers lined up upon project completion. Said another way, the lender and equity investors want the best possible return for the least amount of risk—don't we all?

In the previous sections and chapters we discussed the developer, the development team, and the project tenants. We discussed the four basic phases of most CRE greenfield development projects, some of the specific issues associated with each, finally we discussed location. The location or the where principle represents the general market, target market, and comparable competitive data associated with the location of the project. Now, we come to the why. Why is a unique mix of the who, what, and where principles of commercial real estate development. When we get to why we must demonstrate to the construction lender, equity investors, tenants, teaming partners, community leaders, and others that this project makes good sense and is worthy of their time, money, and effort.

In the why section, we will take all of the information we gathered in the who, what, and where sections of the outline and put them in a form that is easy to read and understand. The why section guides the developer in understanding and creating a *project plan, project budget, financing analysis, and profit analysis.* The why section is the chance to demonstrate that the proposed project will meet the different investment and profit expectations of the investors and, of course, meet the goals and objectives of the developer. It explains why the project will succeed. After all, you want to be proud of what you are creating; bring value to the investors, tenants, the community, and teaming partners; and even make some money for your effort.

We will examine the project plan in four parts: *project budget, financing analysis, profit analysis, and finally a project plan summary.*

Chapter 7: Project Budget

The project budget is an organized look at the various costs associated with getting the project completed, built, and stabilized. There are some simple concepts related to cost that need to be considered, including control of the site by buying, leasing, or partnering with the landowner; project designed, accessible, and built; tenants moved in and paying rent; and paying for or financing all these costs. The developer must organize these items into a simple, easy-to-follow budget presentation. A project budget for a new real estate development can be broken down to five basic areas: land costs, hard construction costs, soft costs, tenant improvement costs, and financing costs. Although there are infinite ways to approach a development cost budget analyzing these five areas of costs should add up to a reliable real estate development project budget.

Finally, it is important to present the cost data in a way that makes sense to the tenants, teaming partners, and the expectation of the debt and equity. To do this, the data is normally presented in a cost per square foot as the common denominator for each budget line item. Since cost per square foot is a typical denominator in the real estate market, the architect, GC, real estate broker, and others will likely present data to you in this fashion. To do the cost-per-square-foot analysis, we must first know all the quantities in terms of square feet.

1 LAND COST

This means, for example, we need to convert the land or land area to build (including needed parking) from acres to feet. Once we have the total area for the specific development and the known net cost of the total land area, we can derive the *land cost per foot* and be in a position to break it down by components of the development. Of course, you then follow the same process for the other project budget cost areas (hard costs, soft costs, TI, and financing costs).

The land cost then is merely the price paid for the land, including expenses incurred to close on the due diligence and purchase of the land presented on a cost per square foot basis.

Development Cost Analysis			
Land/Building Analysis			
	Quantity/Sq. Ft.	Unit Cost	Total
Land Area	4.4acres		
Gross Land Cost	192,100sf	$6.00	$1,152,598
Partner Buyout			
Net Land - Cost	192,100sf	$6.00	$1,152,598
Gross Building Area/$ per Building Ft.	32,500	$35.46	

Table 4: Example of Land Cost Analysis: Unit Cost per Square Foot

2 HARD COSTS

The bulk of the hard costs consist of the building *core, shell, and site work*. The site work can be broken down to both *on-site work and off-site work*. The core and shell construction hard costs consist of all the structural, mechanical, electrical, and plumbing that result in the building. The main categories that make up the hard costs are referred to as *divisions*, and in the construction world there are typically sixteen divisions. These divisions are:

- Division 01-General Conditions
- Division 02-Site Construction
- Division 03-Concrete
- Division 04-Masonry
- Division 05-Metals
- Division 06-Wood and Plastic
- Division 07-Thermal and Moisture Protection
- Division 08-Door and Windows
- Division 09-Finishes
- Divsion 10-Specialties
- Division 11-Equipment
- Divsion 12-Furnishings
- Division 13-Special Construction
- Division 14-Conveying Systems
- Division 15-Mechanical
- Division 16-Electrical

If the GC includes a seventeenth division in his cost analysis, the costs are typically related to fees or special charges. All of the hard costs, broken down by division, should add up to the *contract sum*. The GC is contracted to deliver the project as defined by the architect's plans for the contract sum.

Site work cost is typically broken down into two major components—on- and off-site costs. The off-site costs are costs related to things like laying and connecting utilities and artery and roadway changes, roadway additions, including entrances and exits, curb cuts, drainage and retention, sidewalks, and signage. The on-site costs can be very similar, including utilities, roadway, drainage, and signage. They can also include ground clearing, site preparation, and water retention. These on- and off-site costs and actions are generally the first to happen on any new project construction. It is important to note that the construction lender will typically not fund off-site costs. These costs must be funded out of developer equity. If you think about it this makes sense because there is no way for the construction lender to get a first lien on off-site cost and therefore they would basically be unsecured in this portion of the investment.

The GC will estimate the total of the on- and off-site costs and hard costs until they go to *hard bid* (usually triggered by the closing the construction loan). With the hard bid, the cost of the building supplies and services becomes more certain. The GC should bid each item to three or more subcontractors and suppliers; it's hoped that this will result in savings and reliable budget numbers. (See the earlier discussion of how to bid out TI work.) Depending on the contract type with the GC the estimates for the construction work the hard costs estimate budget might also include a *contingency amount and GC fee.* This contingency amount is an acceptable "fudge" factor to allow for changes, price fluctuations, and mistakes made by the GC, architect, or others on the team in creating, estimating, and bidding the job. The contingency for hard costs and the GC fee respectively, range from 3 to 6 percent of the total hard cost budget. Finally, pay close attention to the GC, *general conditions* (see division 1). It's generally a good idea to ask for a detailed breakdown of the items in the *general conditions.* The GC might be tempted to put corporate overhead and other negotiable items in this division.

Once the land has been purchased and the GC's hard bid costs estimates are complete, we move on to the architects fees, engineering costs, lawyers, city fees, developer fees, and all the predevelopment expenses that have been incurred.

Hard Cost			
Building Shell	32,500	**$102.50**	$3,331,250.00
Site Work		*Included*	
Offsite Costs		*Included*	
Hard Cost Contingency		5%	$166,562.50
Sub-Total Hard Costs		**$107.63**	**$3,497,813**

Table 5: Example of Simple Hard-Cost Budget

3 SOFT COSTS

The soft costs of a typical construction project can be broken down and presented in many ways. We will break them into four main areas: fees, insurance cost, carrying costs, and finally a contingency cost line item.

First, the fee-based work and costs; fee-based expenses make up the bulk of the overall soft-cost expenses of a CRE project, the most common of which are architectural, civil engineering, construction management, legal, and the developer fee. In addition, you will pay a fee for the different *building permits* needed and *impact or tap fees* to the city for connecting to the different utilities. It's important to discuss impact fees with the GC, engineer, and/or architect; the charge for impact fees is often based on the size or diameter of the utility attachment. There are also fees to be paid for the different reports and studies that were discussed in the what and the where sections. You will need to budget to pay all of the fees for the project, including those incurred by the lender and equity provider. Finally, let's not forget the predevelopment expenses. Most lenders will allow you to recover reasonable expenses that you incurred bringing the project to the construction phase in the first pay application and draw request the. Keep good records and document the project-related reason for each expense, and they should be reimbursed in the first draw.

Insurance coverage associated with a new development project is typically referred to as *builder's risk*. The developer is expected to bind liability coverage and *builder's risk insurance* specifically for coverage during the construction of the project and maintain through tenant improvement construction. Once the final *certificate of occupancy* is issued and the tenants move in, the exposure changes and insurance coverage typically converts to a combined policy that covers the property and liability to the building.

Another type of insurance you need to budget for in the soft-costs expense is the *title policy insurance or owners policy title insurance*. The title policy is there to provide protection against title defects to the land that were unknown to you at the time the policy was purchased. The title company will do a complete check for defects and exceptions in the property title and is charged with defending the title when claims are made that are covered by the policy. The title company is responsible for the covered losses limited only by the terms and amounts of the policy. There are typically two types of policies one can purchase—an *owner's policy* and a *lender's policy.* The owner's policy is described above. The lender's policy, sometimes called a loan policy, is issued only to mortgage lenders and is written so it can follow assignment or purchase of the mortgage loan. Many states also have a *construction loan title policy,* which is title insurance for construction loans; this type of policy often requires the *date down endorsement we* touched on in the equity discussion of the *how* chapter. The lender and equity provider will require the appropriate title policy insurance and a clean title before they fund. A clean title is one free of all liens and encumbrances except those acceptable to the first lien holder (the lender).

The third category of soft costs to be budgeted involves estimating certain *carrying costs.* The most common carry costs that must be estimated and budgeted for in the soft-cost category are *lease-up carry, property-tax carry, and land-cost carry.* These costs are labeled carried costs because you are estimating the cost based on certain assumptions. As the developer, you know these carry costs will be incurred, but you don't know exactly when they will be incurred or exactly how much they will be. The ability to pay for them is based on how much is budgeted in the construction loan versus when the tenants begin paying rent over and above financing cost. This leads us right to the *lease-up carry cost.* The estimated lease-up carry cost is the estimate of the timing of when tenants will actually begin paying rent and when this rental income will be enough to fund the triple-net expenses and other costs like interest payments on the construction loan. Realistically unless there is a large single user like the sports bar and restaurant tenant, landlords typically identify, negotiate, and get tenants moved into multitenant buildings over a reasonable period of time. In a multitenant building, tenants don't normally cooperate and move in all at once and start paying rent all at the same time. When you get around to budgeting estimates for the lease up carry, remember to review the tenant lease agreements for anticipated *free rent* and previously agreed upon time schedules for *rent commencement.* When rent commences is typically an area of concern for tenants and an area you are likely to be tempted to negotiate away in the early stages of negotiations with the tenant. However, try to keep rent commencement requirements in the tenant leases consistent and as close to completion of core and shell as possible. In a multitenant building, this unified approach to rent commencement will help you accurately estimate anticipated cash flow (rent) and will keep you, the tenants, and contractors focused on getting the tenant TI completed, and tenants into the building and paying rent.

The other carry costs are similar in nature and must be estimated and paid for by the construction loan proceeds until rent can take over and pay these expenses. As the owner of the project, the developer will at one point have to begin paying property tax and other land carry costs. This may happen before the rent paying tenants cover the basic operating costs. Thankfully, you will have read this book and will know to budget for lease up carry costs and to use the construction loan, soft-costs budget to accrue and pay for these items.

Finally, after budgeting for fees, insurance, and carry costs, it is acceptable to build in a *contingency for soft costs*. The *soft costs contingency* is typically 3-5 percent of the total estimated soft cost budget. This contingency, like the hard costs contingency is to allow for unanticipated changes, fluctuations, or mistakes in the original budget estimates. In addition to the soft-costs contingency you may want to include a miscellaneous budget line item for travel, lodging, certain overhead expenses like marketing and sales. The miscellaneous line item is often an area that the debt and equity will want to review. They expect the developer to cover general business overhead and not charge it specifically to the project. However, you can often get approval for costs that may look like developer overhead if it can be demonstrated the expenses are a direct benefit to the actual project being funded (trade shows, brochures, travel, etc).

Soft Cost			
Architectural & Engineering	5.6%	$6.00	$195,000
Tap Fees		$2.50	$81,250
Legal Fees		$2.31	$75,000
Bank Fees & Appraisal		$0.25	$81,25
Title Insurance		$1.68	$54,450
Advertising & Marketing		$1.00	$32,500
Travel		$0.18	$6,000
Carry Cost (6 Month Carry based on $8/sf)		$4.00	$130,000
Property Tax Carry		$1.25	$40,625
Contingency		3.0%	$166,769
Developer Fee		5.25%	$285,607
Sub-Total Soft Cost		$33.09	$1,075,326
Total Hard & Soft Cost		$140.71	$4,573,139
Total Hard, Soft and Land Cost		$176.18	$5,725,736

Table 6: Simple Soft-Cost Budget Analysis and Subtotals

4 TENANT IMPROVEMENT COSTS

As pointed out earlier, there are numerous ways to present the project budget that is needed to complete a development/construction project. The project budget shown in this book separates *tenant improvement allowance,* along with the projected leasing commissions paid to brokers into a new category labeled tenant improvement costs. Generally, we do this because these expenses tend to relate directly to the leasing of the space and reflect transition from the construction phase to management or operational phase. In addition we need to track the TI allowance closely so we know when the landlord TI allowance has been used, and the tenant becomes responsible for future payment. In the who and what sections we discussed tenant lease up and the need to offer tenant improvement dollars that you, the landlord, pays and not the tenant. This is referred to as the landlord, TI allowance. Therefore, the TI cost is the budgeted projection of the amount of TI allowance paid for by the landlord to get the tenants in the building. Don't forget to budget the landlord management fee for oversight of the TI construction as part of the TI allowance costs. The fee is typically 3-6 percent of the landlord TI allowance amount. As pointed out previously, the landlord TI allowance is rarely enough to pay for all the construction improvement needed for the tenant space plan. The tenant will typically need to invest in the TI to get the space completely built out and ready to use In the who section we discussed the need to get a parent company or owner guarantee of the lease agreement. One possible compromise to full performance guarantee to the lease agreement is to get the parent company or owner to guarantee any TI allowance expended by the developer, however this is merely a potential compromise not the preferred approach. One additional issue to consider the tenant lease agreement needs to clearly delineate when the core and shell of the building is finished and the TI begins. This clear delineation is the best way for the developer and the tenant to know when the TI allowance kicks in and the building structure stops. See the discussion in the what section related to warm, cold vanilla and white shells. Finally, it is important to carefully track the landlord TI allowance for each specific tenant with each monthly pay application and draw request, so that you pay no more and no less than the agreed upon amount.

5 FINANCING INCREMENTAL TENANT IMPROVEMENT COSTS

Most of the time, the cost of the TI needed by a tenant to move into a new building exceeds the landlord TI allowance. The tenant would be responsible for paying the additional TI out of pocket. The tenant and the tenant's broker will usually try to negotiate the amount of landlord TI allowance as part of the overall LOI or lease agreement commitment, but the tenant may realize later that the TI costs will exceed that commitment. The tenant might approach the developer for help covering the additional costs. Developer/landlords are often asked to finance the incremental TI—something that can be tricky. If it is not addressed in the original budget, financing incremental TI may require going back to the lender and/or equity provider to discuss the merits of the proposed financing and investment of additional debt and equity dollars. Signing up a good long-term tenant can hinge on incremental TI. In addition it will mean additional cash flow to the project because you will add incremental TI to the rent along with a finance charge. Financing the incremental TI also adds to the developer/landlord risk equation because the developer is now even more reliant on the success of that tenant.

If you can fund incremental TI, you will want to amortize the total cost of the incremental TI into equal installments as additional rent over, no longer than the primary term of the lease. You must add an acceleration clause for the tenant to pay back incremental TI if there is an early out provision or *escape clause* in the lease agreement. As mentioned, you will want to add to any incremental TI that is funded by the developer, a finance charge. This finance charge should be no less than the project capital stack (cost of money), which is a blended rate of the cost of the equity and debt. Finally, it is almost always a good idea to have the tenant put some of his own cash into the TI. Investing in the TI is additional proof the tenant plans to stay long term and honor the lease agreement.

It is also a good idea to precondition the tenants that the lender for the construction loan might want them to invest their TI contribution with a lump sum or at a minimum on a pro-rata basis with each draw as landlord TI is invested. This TI investment by the tenant, which is often a very substantial sum is the tenant version of the skin-in-the-game principle.

The tenant isn't the only one who will be expected to put skin in the game. If additional capital is needed to fund the incremental TI and the financing wasn't built into the construction budget, the developer may also need to put up additional money. See the discussion of developer coinvestment in this book.

Tenant Improvements, Commissions & Financing Cost		
Leasing Commissions (10 yrs @4.5%)	4.50%	$268,406
Tenant Improvements (Base)	$25.00	$812,500
Sub-Total Development Cost	$209.44	$6,806,643
Financing Cost	$6.48	$210,515
Total Development Cost		
Total Development Cost	$215.91	$7,017,157

Table 7: Example of Tenant Improvement, Commissions, and Financing Cost

6 FINANCING AND INTEREST COSTS

The financing and interest costs consist primarily of the interest payments to the lender for the construction loan and related costs that must be paid to the lender during the construction and lease-up period. As addressed in the who section, the construction loan is interest only for the construction/ tenant improvement/lease-up stages and therefore the developer is only budgeting the interest payments.

➥ The difficulty in budgeting for this line item is that you will want to budget as much interest reserve as possible, but the lender and equity provider may resist this attempt to pad the interest reserve, depending on the financial projections in the project plan. The project plan estimates when the building is to be leased up and therefore, when cash would begin flowing. The developer wants as much interest carry as possible to pay the loan amount while trying to lease up the building. Having more interest carry gives the developer more time to lease up the space in the building so that you can continue to pay for the loan. However, the equity provider and lender are looking at the project plan financial pro forma, which reflects when the building will be leased up and cash shoulld be flowing. The investors (debt and equity) look at the requested interest carry line item of the budget and know, based on the projections, how much interest carry is needed before the estimated rent from the tenants generates enough cash to pay the bills. The interest carry reserve is a very important negotiation. Like many things in life, what can go wrong will often go wrong, and you might not lease up the building as quickly as projected. You don't want to run out of money when it comes to paying the lender the interest payment he expects under the construction loan.

7 BUDGET OVERRUNS

What happens if you run out of money in a particular line item of the project budget? No one's perfect, and it can be difficult to estimate all these costs so early in a project's life. One way to deal with cost overruns is to utilize funds from one budgeted line item to cover another line item shortfall. The lender is usually open to allowing access to budgeted funds from one line item to another if they are similar cost, i.e., borrowing from one soft costs line item to make up for overruns in another soft costs line item. You can assure this capability by negotiating *line item* flexibility into the loan agreement.

Another way to pay for a line item overrun is to access the budgeted contingency line item. The lender will typically not question accessing the *soft costs contingency* should it be needed for overruns in other soft costs line items. The same can hold true for the GC recommending the use of the hard costs contingency for issues like change orders or other hard costs line item overruns. However you may draw the attention of the lender and any third-party construction manager that might have been hired if you attempt to utilize hard costs contingency line items for soft costs overruns and vice versa. This action is indicative to highlighting a blown budget line item and should be reviewed.

It is important during the course of construction for the developer to keep an eye on the contingency amounts for both hard and soft costs. This line item tends to be the first one everyone on the team turns to when there is an unplanned expense or *change order*. However take the time to examine each of proposed offsets to the contingency line item during construction. Some charges may be pure misses or mistakes by the architect or GC.

However, if it appears you are going to run short of the overall project budget and need more cash to finish the project, you may need to make a ➡ *capital call*. A capital call is a request for additional investment from the development partners (typically, the developer and the equity investors). The general partner is in charge of making the operating decisions for the partnership including capital calls. In the partnership agreement there will be detailed provisions related to asking all of the partners to put up additional cash. Of course, the developer will be required to put up additional cash as well, so it's best for all concerned to perform to budget and try to avoid a *partnership capital call.*

CHAPTER 8: FINANCING ANALYSIS

With the land cost, hard cost, soft cost, TI cost, and financing cost calculated, you now have the *total development cost* and a good template for the project budget. With the project budget in hand you can now move to the financing analysis for the project. While outlining the different categories of the project budget, we identified some of the areas that require assumptions. As pointed out earlier in the outline, if a development project is a *multitenant complex* the developer has to project when the different tenants will move in and begin paying rent. They typically will not all move in at the same time, and thus you have to project when each tenant will begin to pay rent. This calculation is often referred to as the *lease-up assumption*. The lease-up assumption then becomes a schedule to the financial pro forma and the single most important projection made relative to predicting the *rent roll* or project gross cash flow. Of course, once the tenants are moved in and paying rent, we start to transition to running or operating the project rather than building the project.

1 HOW TO DETERMINE AN APPROPRIATE LEASE RATE

Determining the lease rate for a new development project may not be as easy as it sounds. To determine the appropriate lease rate, the developer must consider all sides to the project equation. The leasing and brokerage side of the equation might want to offer the cheapest lease rate possible with attractive landlord TI allowances and plenty of free rent. The financial analyst side of the equation does not have to leave the comfort of the computer to decide. The lease rate is the total cost of the project (development, construction, and financing cost) multiplied by an acceptable, risk adjusted ROI. This product is then converted to dollars per total rentable square feet in the building. A single tenant building, like the sports bar and restaurant example, may justify a 10 percent ROI. If the total development cost is $10,000,000.00, the product of the two results in $1,000,000.00. If the project were 50,000 square feet, it would result in a base lease rate of $20 a square foot (net of expenses).

However, to keep it simple most developers establish a market-driven lease rate often inserting a market rate into the financial pro forma and adjusting sales price and other variables to achieve the equity investment return. Of course, you then need to make sure the equity return still meets the expectation of the investor, and we will discuss this further in upcoming chapters. In establishing a lease rate, most developers will look to the surrounding market to determine what is a reasonable lease rate for the project, type (what), location (where), and users (who). The methodology for determining a lease rate can also vary dramatically depending on product type. For example, retail lease rates are often based on a landlord-established minimum base rate and a percentage of tenants' gross receipts. As may now be apparent, most of the variables needed to evaluate an appropriate base lease rate have been discussed in the who, what, and where sections. The difficulty comes into play when the different variables do not balance to produce an attractive project from the perspective of the tenant, investor, and developer.

What do you do if the product of the acceptable ROI and the total development cost translates to a $20 triple-net rent rate, but the market rent rate for comparable product is $17 triple net? You will have to justify to the investors and others why future tenants will be willing to pay significantly more to be in the proposed project. The answer will vary with each project, and it is incumbent on the developer to explain this in reasonable terms. Some of the reasons could be no vacancy in the current market, the specific location is in a high-growth market segment, or even the ability of the anchor tenant (like the sports bar and restaurant) to create new tenant demand. However, you may also need to consider finding ways to lower project cost and/or changing the project size or design. This is where many of the difficult design questions will come into play. A green building with large atrium entrance and fountain display may look good but can it survive the scrutiny of cost versus acceptable market rates? Finally, you may need to assess whether or not the expectation of the investor are justified. Finding the appropriate investor with reasonable market-driven expectations is important for the success of any project. However, as mentioned in the who section the ability of the developer to piece together all aspects of a new project and sell or promote these in a positive way to the investors is often the difference between success and failure.

2 OPERATING PRO FORMA

A development project consists of two distinct businesses. The first business is getting the project built and leased up with tenants moved in and paying rent. The second business is managing this new project once tenants are moved in and paying rent. Managing the operations of a commercial real estate development is a pretty straightforward operation. The new project generates revenues and incurs expenses. These revenues consist of the rent the tenant pays to you—the developer, now more appropriately referred to as the *landlord*. However there are different types of rent. The different rent revenues the tenant pays include base rent, triple-net-expense rent, common-area rent, and possibly even the financed incremental TI rent we discussed earlier. Of course, an operating business not only generates revenue but incurs expenses. If the building tenants have all signed NNN (triple net) leases we know that most of the expenses will be passed through to the tenants as additional rent paid to the landlord. However, there may be some costs or expenses not paid by the tenants such as capital-related expenses. Capital costs must be paid for by the landlord. Hopefully after the building generates revenue and all the expenses are paid there is something left over and this something is referred to as *net operating income or NOI.*

Essentially, you will collect all rent types, (the revenue generated by the rent roll), subtract the NNN expenses and other landlord costs from the revenue and the result will be *a* profit or loss. This is often referred to as the *profit and loss statement. The end result of the profit and loss statement is the* project NOI. For purposes of projecting the long-term NOI, you will want to project the net income once all the tenants are moved in. This is often referred to as the *stabilized NOI.* The stabilized NOI assumes the building is full. In a multitenant building full doesn't necessarily mean 100 percent full. It means realistically full. Most lenders, equity providers, and even potential buyers won't analyze the pro forma at 100 percent utility of the rentable space in a multitenant building. They almost always input a *vacancy factor* and usually this vacancy factor is in the range of 5 percent of the total rentable square footage. The vacancy factor is really just an acknowledgement that there will be constant change in the tenant mix; it is a handy way to account for this flux. Keep this in mind when creating the stabilized NOI. Of course, in a single user facility like the sports bar and restaurant the vacancy factor should not apply.

To determine a vacancy factor and other important items you must know certain measurements related to the overall building. To accurately determine these measurements, you must know the building's gross *square footage, rentable square footage, and usable square footage.* In a multitenant building, understanding these different building measurements is important since triple-net expenses and common-area expenses are prorated to the tenants based on the amount of space they are using compared to the total rentable square footage in the building and the floor the tenant occupies.

3 TENANT *LOAD FACTOR* AND RENTABLE VERSUS USABLE SQUARE FOOTAGE

The landlord/developer owns the elevator, common corridors, hallways, general bathrooms, and other areas that everyone will benefit from and use. How are you compensated for constructing and maintaining the building's common areas? It is standard practice to add a factor, stated as a percentage, to the tenants' rent to cover this. The add-on factor, commonly referred to as the *load factor*, is a way to charge the tenants their pro rata share of the building's common areas not just the space they are directly using.

There are numerous ways to calculate the tenant load factor, and they can vary by building type, structure, and floor. To make the load factor calculation, you must know the gross space of the building. The gross space is converted and stated in *gross square footage (GSF).* The GSF must be determined for the entire building and each floor. The team architect can help you determine the gross area of the building and all of the load factor measurements. He will generally derive this by applying standards set by the *Building Owners and Managers Association (BOMA).* BOMA is a great source for building standards such as load factors and other development project insights (see www.boma.org). Generally, the gross square footage (GSF) in the building is a measurement of the total constructed area of the building, even to the outside of the exterior walls. Using the GSF, you can calculate the rentable space for the building and for each floor.

You calculate the rentable square footage (RSF) by subtracting certain physical aspects of the building commonly referred to as penetrations from the GSF. Stairs and elevator shafts are two good examples of penetrations. These penetrations are converted to the square footage space they occupy and are subtracted from the GSF to derive the RSF. Once you have the RSF, you deduct certain other space types to derive the usable space. Usable space types are the common areas. Common areas are space types like the lobby, corridors, equipment rooms, janitor closets, and exterior walls. Once these areas are deducted, you have determined the usable space, which is referred to as usable square footage or USF. This calculation must be done for each floor because the load factor can vary from floor to floor and therefore the factor applied can vary from tenant to tenant, depending on building location and floor. For example there may be a floor in the building with a long hallway. This long hallway is a common corridor and will add to the common space for that floor.

The result of rentable square footage/usable square footage (stated as a percentage) determines the load factor. The load factor is then applied to the base rent and paid as additional rent by the tenant. Finally make sure the team lawyer adds the appropriate load factor language to the lease agreement.

The calculation of the load factor and the elements from which it is determined will often be an area of contention with the tenants. Most tenants understand that a load factor will be applied, but most will also want to see (audit) the way it is determined. The audit is typically done once the TI has been completed but before they move in. The lease agreement should outline how the tenant load factor and its elements can be reviewed by the landlord and tenant. Look for help from the teaming partners, especially the GC, architect, and broker, for maximizing and assessing a fair, market-driven common-area load factor for the building type and location.

Table 11: Load Factor Gross Building Area - code analysis	23,100	23,100	23,100	69,300		
				-		
Gross Square Footage				-	69,300	
				-		
Convert to Rentable SF:				-		
Deduct Penetrations:				-		
Stair 1 Rm 103/203	(180)	(180)	(180)	(540)		
Stair 2 Rm 102/202	(191)	(191)	(191)	(573)		
Elevator Rm 101/201	**(80)**	**(80)**	**(80)**	**(240)**		
Elevator Gurmey	**(120)**	**(120)**	**(120)**	**(360)**		
Three Shaft Penetrations	-	**(183)**	**(183)**	**(366)**		
Rentable Square Feet	**22,529**	**22,346**	**22,346**	**67,221**		
Efficiency %(Gross/Rentable)					97.0%	
Convert to USEABLE-Planned						
Lobby 100/200	**(435)**	**(416)**	**(416)**	**(1,267)**		
Elevator Eq Rm 110	(108)			(108)		
Unisex Toilet 211	-	(74)	(74)	(148)		
Corridor Room 212	**(580)**	(1,248)	(1,248)	(3,076)		
Janitor Rm 214		(72)	(72)	(144)		
Exterior Wall	(314)	(312)	(312)	(938)		
	-	-		-		
Architect's USEABLE SF Approx.	21,092	20,224	20,224	61,540		
R/U Load Factor	**106.8%**	**110.5%**	**110.5%**	**109.2%**		

Table 8: Example of Rentable and Usable Square Footage

We now have a project budget, lease-up assumptions and rent roll (estimated project cash flow) and the net operating income for the stabilized building.

Let's return to our sports bar and restaurant example. The sports bar and restaurant is a single-user tenant and needs 25,000 square feet (as a single user, we will assume the base rent includes any applicable load factor). Let's also assume they have agreed to a ten-

year initial lease term, with a base rent of $12.00 triple net (meaning we will pass through to the tenant as additional rent, maintenance, insurance, and tax expense). The base rent on the 25,000 square feet of space is $300,000 in annual cash rent payments. Finally, our broker has told us that most buildings of this size, use, and in this area of town run about $8 a foot in triple net (NNN) expenses. This triple net payment is estimated each year and paid as additional rent each month. Since this is a single user building, we will assume the utility bills go directly to the tenant. We now have a total of $20 a foot or $500,000 a year in various rent payments. To derive the NOI, we now must subtract from these various rent payments the out-of-pocket costs and expenses we incur to run and manage the building. To make this calculation easy, we will use the triple net expenses of $8 or $200,000. We now have a simple but complete budget from which we derive our NOI. In our case the NOI is gross rent minus expenses or $300,000.

	Total	PSF
Revenue		
Base Rent	$ 300,000	$ 12.00
NNN Expense Reimbursement	$ 200,000	$ 8.00
Total Revenue	$ 500,000	$ 20.00
Expenses		
NNN Expenses	$ 200,000	$ 8.00
Total Expenses		
Net Operating Income	**$ 300,000**	**$ 12.00**

Many developers will also build in a capital expense line item or cap ex to indicate accrual in the operating budget for possible capital expenditures. Capital expenditures are typically not a part of the triple-net expenses passed through to the tenant. However, it is not uncommon for a developer/ landlord in a single-user building to negotiate into the lease agreement that capital expenditures and operating expenses pass through to the tenant. The extreme version of this type of lease is often referred to as an *absolute lease*.

Now to complete the financing analysis, we need at least one more item. We need to pro forma the expectation for long-term debt financing or takeout of the construction financing.

4 LONG-TERM DEBT FINANCING: SALE AND REFINANCING

As we have discussed, the construction loan is short term. Typically, a construction loan is only long enough to get the project built, and tenants moved in and paying rent. Shortly after the tenants begin paying rent you will have to refinance the construction loan to a more permanent loan facility. This may take the form of selling the project to a buyer who will refinance the entire project capital stack. With the *permanent debt* you are modeling in the financing analysis the takeout of the construction lender and the equity provider. You will then model or replace this financing with financing that is typically of much longer term, possibly as long as thirty years. By working with the equity provider, real estate broker, and others you will be able to determine the market rate, term, and other conditions for long-term financing for the project product type and location, and to incorporate this information into the financing projections.

You will need to realize enough money from the long-term debt financing or sale to wipe out the total construction debt and the equity invested principal. In addition, you will hope to sell the project to pay all other expenses and to realize a profit. How does the equity investor get his money back, preferred rate of return, and profit participation?

Let's examine what we have outlined up to this point.

We created a projected project budget so we believe we know our estimated *total development cost*. We created lease-up assumptions and a rent roll so we could estimate the timing of the cash flow, the annual gross cash amount, and when the building would start to stabilize. With this information, we created a pro forma profit and loss statement for the operating business, which resulted in a projected net operating income or NOI.

Finally, we addressed refinancing the construction loan with longer-term financing and paying back the project costs, construction loan, and the principal to the equity investor.

We are able to do this because we assumed in the analysis that we could sell the completed project for a profit. So how do you, the developer/owner/landlord forecast a profit?

CHAPTER 9: THE PROFIT ANALYSIS

So it's late Saturday night. You and the financial analyst teaming partner are trying to finish up the financial projections for the sports bar and restaurant project and the presentation to a prospective equity investor on Monday morning. The projected *project budget and financing analysis* are completed, and now you are trying to complete the final piece that helps make this project worth the effort—the profit analysis. You have to demonstrate to the equity investors that the project makes economic sense and the profit potential meets their investment expectations.

In the how section, we address the investor's concern with the time value of money. How long will the money will be invested before the investor can reasonably expect a return on the investment and what is the estimated return on investment (ROI) the investor can reasonably expect based on the facts you provide about the project and his own due diligence. In the how section we state the following:

➡ You (the developer) will take their money (equity) and use it to get more money from the lender. Using this money, you will buy the land, build the building, fill it with tenants, manage it, and then sell or refinance the finished project. The equity investor will evaluate the risk associated with each of these steps, forecast how long they will take to complete, and then estimate the price for which the finished product could be sold. If you take the core components (how much money is invested, length of time the money will be tied up, net cash received while stabilizing, and how much cash is realized upon sale) and throw these components into a formula and add a *yield*, you can determine the projected *internal rate of return or IRR*. More importantly, the investor can reasonably forecast a rate of return (ROI) that makes the proposed development project attractive to them and one they want to invest in! Most equity investors for startup or *greenfield* CRE development projects expect a total ROI in the 20 percent range.

1 HOLD PERIOD

To complete the profit analysis, we must make a couple of assumptions. The first assumption relates to the length of time the equity investor cash will be invested before realizing a return. This is referred to as the *hold period or investment period*. The hold period is a forecast of how long it will take to complete and sell or refinance the project once the construction loan is closed.

We start with the closing of the construction loan because very few lenders will close the construction loan unless the building permits have been pulled or just ready to be pulled and construction can start. Construction lenders will only lend when the permit is pulled because of a concern that their first lien interest may somehow be impaired if they begin funding too early. This concern relates to the fact that once subcontractors begin performing work on a project they begin to accrue a legal lien right to be paid.

We can conveniently determine a reasonable hold period by examining the phases of the development process that take place after loan closing. First we will examine the construction phase, the length of which is dependent on project type, size, and team experience. We'll assume that it will take twelve to fourteen months to complete construction of core, shell, and site improvements. Now, of course, we need to get the tenants moved in and paying rent. Let's refer to this as the TI or stabilization stage and assume for financial modeling purposes this will require a total of twenty to twenty-four months. Moving in tenants includes a separate permit process and build out. As we learned in the discussion or the financing analysis, tenants in a multitenant building won't move in all at once. To recap, we need twelve to fourteen months to construct the core and shell, and an additional twenty to twenty-four months to get all the projected tenants in and paying rent before the project is stabilized. That is an estimated time period of thirty-two months to a stabilized, sellable project. Finally, we need to add about four months to allow time for the project to be sold or refinanced. For purposes of calculating profit you have now developed a thirty-six month hold period that is reasonable and that we can use in the profit analysis.

2 PROFIT ASSUMPTIONS

There are four basic prongs to the profit analysis: how much money is invested, how long will it be invested, how much cash flow has been received during the hold period, and how much money will be realized as a result of selling/refinancing the finished project. For purposes of our calculations, we are assuming a hold period of thirty-six months. In the how section, we address the amount of money that needs to be invested by the equity provider. The lender will typically loan no more than 80 percent of the total project costs. However, in almost every instance 80 percent is on the high end, and you should expect the construction lender to loan closer to 70 percent. For purposes of this book, we will assume a 75 percent, *loan-to-cost* construction loan from the lender. This means that the developer needs to raise the additional 25 percent. We refer to this 25 percent as the equity needed to complete the capital stack for the project, and this equity will include the developer coinvestment.

Let's assume that the total project cost of the sports bar and restaurant is estimated to be $2,000,000. Let's also assume you have initial LOI from a lender for a 75/25 loan to cost. This means that you must raise $500,000 dollars in equity to compliment the $1.5 million the lender will give you for the construction loan (75/25 percent). Therefore, we now know that in order to get our sports bar and restaurant up and running, equity will need to invest $500,000. We believe this equity will be invested for an estimated thirty-six months before it can be sold and refinanced. Let's not forget the developer coinvestment or contribution to equity. As we discuss in the how section of the outline the developer coinvestment is typically 5-10 percent of the total equity needed. For purposes of this example, let's assume you will need to contribute $50,000 or 10 percent of the total equity needed.

	Total	Percent
loan	1,500000	75%
Required Equity	500,000	25%
Total Cost	2,000,000	100%
Investor	450,000	90%
Developer	50,000	10%
Required Equity	500,000	100%

In our model the developer has to come up with $50,000 or ten percent of the required equity. ➥ As mentioned in the how chapter, the developer can often utilize a portion of the developer fee to pay for the developer coinvestment. (note the tax implications of this approach.) The developer fee is typically anywhere from 3-6 percent of the total cost for the project. So for a $2,000,000 project like our sports bar and restaurant, we will assume a 4 percent fee or $80,000. This means you would utilize $50,000 of the developer fee as the developer coinvestment and receive the other $30,000 dispersed in equal amounts over the estimated life of the construction and paid out with each monthly draw request.

We now know the amount of equity needed to invest and the estimated time period it will be invested. To complete our financial analysis, we need to determine the projected return upon sale.

3 PROFIT ANALYSIS, DISCOUNTED CASH FLOW, AND CAP RATES

We are finally at the last leg of estimating the potential profits of the project. We know our total project cost ($2,000,000.00), we have a pro forma for how and when the rent will be received ($500,000.00 annually), we have the projected annual operating and management costs ($200,000.00), and we've determined the annual net operating income ($300,000.00). Since we have a LOI from the bank, we know how much cash we can expect from our lender (75/25 percent loan to cost or $1,500,000.00) and therefore how much we need in equity to complete our capital stack ($500,000.00). Finally, with the hold period calculation (thirty-six months), we have a reasonable feel for how long the debt and equity will remain invested before sale or refinancing might occur.

So how do we take this information and determine the gain or profit from the sale of our successful commercial real estate development project?

Commercial real estate is typically bought and sold using two valuation methods. The *discounted cash flow (DCF)* method and the *capitalization rate* method or better known as the *cap rate* method. For the discounted cash flow method one of the important variables to calculate the DCF is the future cash flow of the tenants rent, net of out-of- pocket expenses to run the building, plus a *residual value*, which is the value of the underlying real estate improvement. The easiest way to think of the residual value is as the estimated value of the real estate at the time of sale. Once the developer has estimated the cash flow from the rent tenants will pay the DCF can be determined by discounting this cash flow by a *risk adjusted required rate of return*. This is referred to as *present valuing* the future net cash flow, which then results in the DCF. *Present valuing* is the process of estimating all future cash flow, applying a discount factor (usually at the applicable cost of capital) to determine the present value of the cash flow. You may also us these cash flow to calculate the IRR.

However, probably the most common way to value commercial real estate is to apply the appropriate cap rate or to utilize the capitalization method. The *cap rate* is the current yield or the first full year's net rent (income) over the property value and stated as a percent. Here are the formulas:

➡️ **Cap Rate = Net Operating Income (NOI)/Property Value**

➡️ **Property Value = Net Operating Income/Cap Rate**

➡️ **Net Operating Income = Property Value x Cap Rate**

The appropriate cap rate is derived by researching comparable historical sales of properties or projects similar to the project you are building and selling. By looking at the cap rates that were applied to comparable projects, you can begin to get comfortable that the buyers for similar projects will purchase a project applying the same or a similar cap rate. This is one of the primary reasons we needed the comparable and competitive market data discussed in the where section of the outline. For purposes of attracting equity investors to invest in the project, you will want to work with the teaming partner broker and others, including the targeted equity investor, to help determine the comparable cap rates for the product type, tenant mix, and location. Once you have a supportable cap rate and the annual NOI for the project, you can determine a reasonable projected purchase price for the project using the formulas given above.

It's now even later on Saturday night, and you and the team financial analyst are trying to finish up the profit analysis for the sports bar and restaurant financial model. You have plugged the many assumptions we detailed in the previous chapters into a financial spreadsheet and have applied one of the formulas given above to derive the *deal return*.

To simplify the deal return formula, we will assume no excess cash flow was distributable or accumulated from operations for the hold period. The deal return is the overall profit net of paying back the lender principal and the cost of the refinancing. From the equity investor's perspective, it's the dollars in (invested) and the dollars out (return). Using the sports bar *and restaurant figures we determined earlier, we know we invested $500,000.00 in equity. Based on our due diligence, we believe that a cap rate of 11 percent is supportable and the appropriate cap rate for our product type and location. The cap rate is applied to first full year net income or NOI, which we projected to be $300,000. The projected NOI ($300,000) divided by the cap rate (11 percent) results in gross sales proceeds of $2,727,273.00. From the $2,727,273.00 we would subtract our cost of the sale (let's assume $100,000.00) and pay back the lender principle ($1,500,000). Remember, we have been paying the interest during construction and stabilization. The deal profit would then be $1,127,273.00. Therefore, from the perspective of the equity investor, the dollars in would be $500,000 and the dollars out (the dollars available for distribution) would be $1,127,273.00.*

Net Operating Income	$ 300,000
Cap Rate	11.0%
Gross Sales Proceeds	$2,727,273
Cost of Sale	$(100,000)
Net Sales Proceeds	$2,627,273
Current Loan	$1,500,000
Net Distributable Proceeds	$1,127,273

Now, based on the waterfall in the partnership agreement, let's determine how the deal return gets distributed!

4 WATERFALL, DISTRIBUTION OF PROFITS AND SUMMARY FINANCIALS

Once you have the deal return amount, you can begin to apply the cash or net distributable proceeds to the waterfall. (The waterfall is described in more detail in the how section.) The waterfall sets out the priority for cash distributions and is typically outlined in the partnership agreement between the developer and the equity investor. First, of course, you pay all costs and expenses and the lender the full amount due under the loan ($1,600,000.00). Next, the equity investors expect to get their investment back, plus a pref. A pref is a preferred return on the invested equity. For purposes of this outline, we will assume the equity investor invested $450,000.00 for thirty-six months, and you agreed to pay them a 9 percent preferred return. Of course, this means you have invested $50,000 for thirty-six months also at a 9 percent preferred rate of return (90/10 percent). So the equity and the developer (you) get invested principal back plus a pref. Finally, you look to the waterfall provisions of the partnership agreement to determine how the remaining funds get distributed.

In our example, 9 percent invested over thirty-six months on $500,000 would equate to additional distribution or pref to the equity investors of $147,515. The deal return then gets reduced by $647,515 by distributing this amount to the equity investors. This leaves us with $479,758 left to distribute. As mentioned above, to determine the remaining waterfall or priority of distribution you would look to the partnership agreements. We will assume the partnership agreement outlines equal distribution of profits and no clawback provisions. (See the how section for more detail on clawback.) Therefore, the remaining deal return would be distributed 50/50 percent or $239,879 to the equity investor and to the developer (you). Of course, you must now complete the overall analysis and assessment of financial return to the investors by calculating the IRR and present this information in a complete financial summary. One final point important to the developer; you will recall in our example the developer contributed $50,000 to the equity capital. In our example the developer did this by deferring the receipt of a portion of the developer fee. At some point the deferred developer fee will become earned or payable-typically based on some specific performance criteria related to the project; the issuance of certificate of completion or tenants starting to pay rent.. Once the developer fee is earned or payable it becomes taxable although the developer will not have actually received any cash. This can result in a cash or liquidity problem for the developer come tax time.

The deal return summary is as follows:

			Year 1	Year 2	Year 3	Total
Initial Investment			500,000,00			500,000.00
Preferred Return		9%	45,000.00	49,050.00	53,464.50	147,514.50
		Year 0	Year 1	Year 2	Year 3	
Initial investment		(500,000)				
Cash Flow			-	-	1,127,273	
Investor Cash Flow						
Initial Investment		(500,000)				
Preferred Return	9%		45,000	49,050	53,465	
Cumulative Preferred			45,000	94,050	147,515	
Preferred Paid					147,515	
Return of Capital					500,000	
Cash Flow to Distribute					479,758	
Profit Split						
Investor	50%				239,879	
Developer	50%				239,879	
Investor Pro-Rata Cash Flow		(450,000.0)	-	-	822,642	
Developer Pro-Rata Cash Flow		(50,000.0)	-	-	304,631	
		Investor	Developer			
Dollars In		450,000	50,000			
Dollars Out		822,642	304,631			
Profit		372,342	254,631			
Multiple		1.83x	6.09x			
IRR		22.3%	82.6%			

Table 9: Deal Return Summary.

To end the long Saturday night and prepare for Monday morning's presentation to the potential equity investors, you need to take the project budget, financing analysis and profit analysis and put that information in a form that is attractive and can be easily read and understood—the *project plan*.

CHAPTER 10: THE PROJECT PLAN

INTRODUCTION

In the who chapter, we discussed the important components of a business plan that tells the world about the developer and outlines the development business the developer represents. The project plan is the business plan for the specific development project you are going to build. It is the most visible sales and marketing tool for attracting debt, equity, team members, and community support. ➡ The project plan is also a written negotiation. It is a detailed look at the project and the project's potential. Therefore, it represents an outline of what the developer is willing to trade or give up in value in exchange for the equity investment and even construction loan. For example, if you include a 10 percent preferred return for the investors in the financial analysis, the likely starting point for negotiation with investors will be 10 percent. This is very important to keep in mind as you prepare to put the project plan in front of potential investors and partners. You want the project plan to be attractive enough to encourage investment and at the same time to build in room to negotiate while maintaining an attractive rate of return for the developer (you).

You will need to have a project plan along with the project budget, financing analysis, and profit analysis we just discussed. The project plan is your best chance for the developer to present the project vision and how this vision is transformed to a completed development. As is the case with many of the items we have addressed, there are literally hundreds of ways to present a project plan. However, almost all project plans no matter how presented will contain the basic information we have discussed and examined in of the who, what, where, why, and how chapters of this book.

Let's review the project components we've addressed so far, and see how they factor in the project plan: ➡

WHO: means the developer, the development team members, and most importantly the tenant(s) committed to the project.

WHAT: defines the four basic phases of a typical greenfield development project (vision/pre-development, construction, management and sale/refinancing), and then addresses issues concerning what is specifically being built and the suitability of the chosen site for what is being built. The what section considers whether you can build what you want to build on the chosen site.

WHERE: reflects the real estate mantra of location, location, location for the chosen site and analyzes the market with a specific detailed look and analysis of the general area, target area, site analysis, and the relevant demographics, comparable competitive projects, and specifics associated with these comparable competitive projects.

WHY: utilizes all of the key points addressed in the who, what, and where sections to pull together the necessary elements of the project budget, financing analysis, and profit analysis to justify and encourage investment in the project,

How: the process of understanding, preparing, presenting, and ultimately procuring the construction debt and equity investment needed to get the vision and predevelopment effort financed and the project built, operated, stabilized, and possibly refinanced or sold.

So, all we need do now is gather all we've learned, assembled, and created in the course of this book, and put it into an informative, compelling project plan.

1 KEY COMPONENTS OF A PROJECT PLAN

Most project plans, regardless of property type, location, or design will include and address the following components:

Cover page and table of contents: the plan will likely start with a cover page that shows a graphic of the location and a rendering or picture of the site or existing facility; it is followed by a detailed table of contents.

Legal disclaimer: the project plan is NOT an *investment prospectus* and should make it clear that there are assumptions and risks associated with investing in the proposed project. You can find many examples of appropriate legal disclaimers on the Internet and, of course, the legal teaming partner will be happy to supply one for you.

Project plan, opening summary, and executive summary: ➡ every project plan should start with a good summary that explains what are you going to build, where are you building, and who are you building it for. Try to keep it to one or two pages if possible and cover the most important aspects of the key information. You can combine the project plan summary with other essentials and provide greater detail to create an executive summary. An executive summary is just a condensed version of the entire project plan.

Project plan overview: this section reiterates what is discussed in the project plan summary but in significantly greater detail. The overview is essentially a detailed look at the various aspects of the development-. It will describe in detail the developer, the team, and the experience level of each member, especially as it relates to the project, product type, and location. The plan should also discuss in detail the single-user tenant or tenant mix, their background, experience, financial strength (including the guarantors), and summary of the legal commitment as it relates to the project.

The overview should describe in detail the proposed project and its use. When describing the project you will need to touch on all four phases discussed in the what section. The project plan overview should address specific descriptions of the components parts of the development; status of the acquisition of the land; and description of site issues (environmental, survey, title, on- and off-site issues, permits, and others). If an initial environmental report exists, you should attach reports on survey, plat, soils, utilities, etc. You will want to include as many reports and other visual aids as possible; this could include ground and aerial photos of the site and maps showing the area surrounding the site. ➡ The project plan is the developer's best written/digital shot at describing the project and because of this fact, it is a powerful sales and marketing tool. Don't hesitate to make it visually attractive and easy to read. You could include a graphic, map, photo, or rendering/conceptual drawings if possible. Potential equity investors and potential lenders see hundreds of development proposals, so you need to do what you can to make them want to read and focus on yours.

The project plan overview needs to address the location and the demographics associated with the location. Attach as much market information as you, the broker, the other teaming partners and the Internet can provide. If a third-party marketing study has been done, it should be attached. Explain in detail why the specific site is a good one for the project type and the tenant mix. With the location and demographics, you will also want to include the information described in the where chapter, including the general area analysis, target area analysis, and specific use analysis. With the specific use analysis, you will include information on comparable projects and data related to the competition. In conjunction with this demographic data, you will want to discuss in detail aspects of the location that directly relate to leasing the *speculative space or "spec" space,* which is the uncommitted space in the building. Securing committed tenants and the strong likelihood that the spec space will be leased in a timely manner and within the terms outlined in the financial plan are extremely important in procuring the financing commitment.

You will need to include an outline of the proposed ownership structure between the developer and the investors, and a description of proposed deal. The ownership structure can be in the form of a corporate hierarchy and should indicate ownership percentages and general partners when applicable. It is also a good idea to create an investment summary or *financial summary.* The financial summary should consist of a summary of the project budget, financing analysis, and profit analysis. The summary should provide cost estimates, financing pro forma, profit projections, and describe the proposed waterfall of cash upon refinancing or sale. Once you have completed the project plan, you will want to attach the financial summary, as well as the complete project budget, financial analysis, and profit analysis.

Finally, If possible you will want to tailor the project plan to the reader. Most commercial real estate investment groups have a Web site that will typically outline the firm's strategy, goals, and objectives. Find a way to tailor the project plan to highlight how the project meets or exceeds these goals and objectives. Drawing a closer line between what you want to do and what potential investors want to invest in will make the investors more receptive to what you are proposing and more willing to invest.

"WHY"

(Section Review)

The Why Principle guides the developer in understanding and creating a *Project Plan and Financial Analysis. The Financial Analysis can be broken down into Project Budget, "Financing" Analysis and Profit Analysis.*

1 Project Budget

Total Development costs; Land cost, Hard costs, Soft costs, Tenant Improvement cost, Financing costs and dealing with budget overruns.

2 Financing Analysis

Lease Rates, Load Factors, Operating Pro Forma, Long term Financing Options.

3 Profit Analysis

Hold Period, Profit Assumptions, Discounted Cash Flows and Cap Rates, Cap Formulas, Cash "Waterfall".

4 The Project Plan

PART 5:
THE HOW PRINCIPLE
How to Get the Project Financed and Built: Read the last section first?

In this section:

This book anticipates the involvement of commercial bank debt for the construction loan and commercial real estate equity investors for the equity. These two market-driven entities will force the developer to ask and answer most if not all the most important questions needed to be asked and answered to get a new commercial real estate development project built and open for business.

INTRODUCTION

The real estate mantra *location, location, location* might well be changed to *finance, finance, finance*. Barring a rich parent or relative, getting the financing, investment, or cash needed to develop a commercial real estate project outlines the entire process of the who, what, where, why, and how principles to get a project built.

This ➡ book is based on the theory that meeting the needs and demands of potential financing partners will force the developer to ask and answer all of the critical questions to move a new CRE development project forward. Getting someone to finance a project with both *debt and equity* (sometimes referred to as the *capital stack*) addresses most if not all of the critical questions that need to be asked and answered to put a project on the right path for success.

Chapter 11: The Construction Loan or Debt Lender

1 LOAN PROCESS

All projects take money. One must acquire the land, pay for certain up-front costs and expenses, pay to get the project built, and pay to support the building while finding enough tenants to fill it. This book explores in detail the requirements and perspective of unrelated construction lenders and investors as they consider request to fund a development project.

Almost all commercial real estate construction projects are financed by a majority of debt. The debt is usually in the form of a construction loan from a commercial bank and depending on the tenants, location, property type, and market forces at the time, the debt will normally constitute somewhere between 65-75 percent of the projected *project cost or value*. The debt financing, which is expressed as a percentage of the total amount of money needed to build a project, will be largely determined by the preleasing levels and intended equity contribution. Initially one will seek from the bank a term sheet more commonly referred to as a *letter of interest or intent* (LOI). To get to the LOI, the developer will need to supply the lender with certain basic information from which the bank can make an initial determination that the project is of interest to them and within the bounds of their *underwriting*. One of the most important criteria for the construction lender is the *project plan and financial summary*. These documents will determine, amongst other things, the overall estimated project cost and, therefore, the initial estimate of how much money is needed to build the project. However, the LOI from a prospective construction lender will give you an initial estimate of the terms on which the bank will lend to build the project. The LOI is something tangible to show to the equity investors and other interested parties that the project is feasible or more importantly, worthy of being financed. Once the debt amount of the capital stack is determined, you have determined the amount of equity you will need. Of course, this can work in both directions. Often the lender will want to see the equity commitment as part of his LOI review, and the equity investor will want to see the lender's LOI. In either event the developer needs to work with the potential debt providers and equity investors simultaneously to reach the goal of obtaining the total project financing needed.

2. PROJECT APPRAISAL

Ultimately, for the bank to determine a reasonable cost or value for a project, they will commission an *appraisal* by a third-party independent *licensed appraiser* (that the developer gets to pay for). The appraisal for the project will help determine the estimated market value and, therefore, largely determine the amount of debt you can expect to support the financing. In most instances an appraisal for a new development project will be a *plans and specs appraisal*. It is called a plans and specs appraisal because the project is not yet built and other than the land and the developer's vision (translated to the architect's plans and specs) there is nothing tangible to appraise. To conduct an appraisal, the appraiser will assess the surrounding existing *comparable projects* (*comps*). To determine whether a project is comparable to the planned project, the appraiser will look for projects that are similar in use, location, lot size, tenant mix, construction type, and numerous other variables. The appraised value, then, is really the appraiser's opinion of the potential value of the project after utilizing the information gathered and related to the comps. Don't underestimate the importance of the appraoisal. The appraisal is very important in determining the perceived value of the development project and how much money you will be able to borrow.

3 CONSTRUCTION LOAN

The bank, as the primary force behind financing a project, takes a *first lien position* on all the assets of the project. The construction lender is also likely to request a *personal guarantee* on the construction loan and probably even an indemnity for certain exposures like *environmental liability*. Yes, the developer will be asked to guarantee the construction loan. In fact, there are numerous areas of personal and professional exposure and liability that the developer needs to be aware of as he attempts to get the project financed and built.

The construction loan usually is tied to a *floating interest rate* typically associated with the current *prime rate of interest or London Interbank Offered Rate (LIBOR)* and requires interest-only payments during the construction period and a lease-up period after construction completion. The construction loan is typically of short duration (twenty-four to forty-eight months long) and must be refinanced to a miniperm or permanent loan facility at the end of the construction loan term. One unique thing about construction financing is that interest payments due to the bank during the construction period can, and are expected to be, a part of the project budget. In fact, you will want to try and build in the largest *interest reserve* the lenders will allow. Development projects almost always take longer than anticipated, and the lender will never lose sight of the developer's ability to pay the construction loan interest. The lender will also typically charge a *loan origination fee* and often require that the developer pay a *nonrefundable commitment fee* or loan committee review fee. Of course, the developer not only pays these fees but also gets to pay for all costs and expenses associated with the request and closing of the construction loan. All these fees can be budgeted and reimbursed to the developer when the actual loan closes. Another fee item that is typically part of the project budget is the *developer fee*.

4 DEVELOPER FEE

The developer fee is how you get paid for the time and energy you have committed and will commit to the project, specifically in the vision and predevelopment stages. The other way the developer gets paid for his efforts is when the project is sold for a *profit* or collects rent over and above total cost and expenses (also a form of profit). ➡ The developer fee typically ranges anywhere from 3-6 percent of the overall projected cost of the project (including, in some cases, the cost of the land). It will get budgeted as part of the *soft costs* of the project budget. The soft costs are costs not directly related to actual construction. As you might guess, the costs associated with the actual construction are referred to as the *hard costs*. The amount of the developer fee, and how and when it will be paid will be negotiated between you and the lender and equity investors. Normally the fee is paid out of the monthly *construction draw* in equal amounts over the estimated life of the construction project. It is also possible to use a portion of the developer fee to pay for the *developer equity contribution* that you will need to make to get the equity investor to invest; more about that later in the book.

5 TENANTS AND THE ➡ IMPORTANCE OF PRELEASING

The single most important criterion to the lender in making the loan is a belief he will be paid back. This will often require proof of substantial *preleasing* of the project or some form of *guaranteed takeout* when the construction loan matures. Most lenders in a good market will expect no less than 50 percent of the available space in the project to be preleased. They are not alone in this expectation; the equity investor will also typically expect substantial preleasing. The reason the investors want to see the pre-leasing commitment is that it represents the best evidence the project will be a success, and they will be paid back.

One of the alternatives to substantial preleasing is a *guaranteed takeout of the construction loan*. There are certain property types such as multifamily (apartments) that rarely prelease. The developer in this type of project will sometimes enhance the lender's position by getting a creditable third party such as a *commercial real estate investment group* to sign a guaranteed takeout of the construction loan at maturity. This type of financing enhancement normally requires a significant track record of success by the developer in the specific project type to be developed; you can expect a heightened level of due diligence from the real estate investment group on the front end of the project and reduced profit participation for the developer upon sale. The good news is that many lenders will fund from 90 to 100 percent of the project cost if the guaranteed takeout group has acceptable credit, capability, and reputation.

6 DEBT SERVICE COVERAGE AND INTEREST COVERAGE RATIOS

As mentioned, most construction lenders will normally require at least 50 percent tenant preleasing commitment before they will lend. The lender wants to see significant tenant commitment before investing because it gives him assurance that the loan will be repaid. In fact, most lenders have a *debt service coverage ratio (DSCR)* or *interest coverage ratio* they require in the precommitment, predevelopment stage. Simply put, this means the bank will analyze the predevelopment lease commitments and determine whether or not you can cover the interest payment on the construction loan. The developer addresses the interest coverage ratio projection in the financial modeling or financing analysis. The debt service coverage ratio or DSCR is technically defined as net cash provided by operating activities, lease, and other payments by the tenants (or precommitted tenants) divided by the average current liabilities associated directly with the construction debt or operations. The interest coverage ratio is merely the ability to pay the interest on the construction loan out of projected net cash flow. If you model an interest coverage ratio of at least one to one (net cash to interest amount due) the lender will likely be satisfied. The interest coverage required by the lender will vary depending on product type, market conditions, and other factors. Finally most lenders for CRE development projects will also apply a *developer net worth covenant*. This covenant compares the developer's personal net worth to the overall loan size.

To summarize, a lender can also be convinced to commit to a construction loan if the developer has: a significant personal net worth, is able to invest substantially more equity in a project than might be expected, has arranged for an acceptable form of guaranteed takeout, or has a significant tenant base committed to the project.

7 GOVERNMENT ENHANCEMENT PROGRAMS

Another form of guarantee that many lenders are attracted to is a government enhancement or guarantee program. Federal Housing Administration (FHA), Housing Urban Development (HUD), United States Department of Agriculture (USDA), Small Business Administration (SBA) and other government agencies have specific programs that can guarantee up to 90 percent of development cost if the project meets the program criteria. Most government programs are related to housing, health care, and/or rural or small business funding programs. Typically, a government supported program is offered in the form of *enhancement*. The government agency will guarantee the loan made by a commercial lender to projects that qualify. Therefore the loan is enhanced, and lenders and even equity providers have incentive to loan or invest in the project because they have assurance the loan or a good portion of the loan will be purchased or assumed. Governments tend to enhance development in areas where they perceive a public benefit. For example, low income housing tax credits are available for defined *qualified census tracts* or *difficult development areas*. The FHA/HUD programs are most often related to affordable housing and/or health care developments, while the FDA and SBA programs are often focused on encouraging investment in rural areas or small business enterprises. There are also federal programs rather than agency-driven enhancement programs. The

New Market Tax Credit program is a good example. In this instance the federal government offers tax incentives for private investors putting capital into *community development entities* that in turn finance development projects in underserved or challenged areas. Simply put, an investor invests a million dollars in a qualifying project and gets one million one hundred thousand dollars in tax credits. Government subsidized *bonds* are often used to encourage investment and new development efforts. Since we are exploring the subject of government enhancement or subsidy, there are also government sponsored programs to set aside government contracts, including development and construction contracts for certain small or disadvantaged businesses. These range from size-standard criteria to socially or economically disadvantaged businesses and individuals. Finally, there is a growing need at the government level to fund countless development projects. Public-private partnerships (PPP or P3s) are becoming the vehicle of choice for joint ventures between private developers and public entities. Typically the developer will build the project and long term lease the facility back to the public entity. Often the public entity owns the facility at the end of the lease term. Suffice to say that researching, federal, state, and even local government programs and agencies for enhancing a commercial real estate development project can be well worth the time and effort.

8 ONE-STOP-SHOP FINANCING ALTERNATIVES

Many long term purchasers of commercial real estate projects also have development finance divisions. These development finance divisions often team up with third-party developers to finance and develop new projects. New CRE development projects are often referred to as *greenfield* developments. *Real estate investment trusts (REITS)* will often team with third-party developers and finance both debt and equity needed for a greenfield development project. Although this may sound compelling, a virtual one-stop shop of commercial real estate finance for financing the entire capital stack of a project comes with a price. If someone is willing to step up and finance the development effort and then purchase or own the completed project, the developer's risk has been greatly reduced, and the value you add has been reduced. Most REIT investors that will finance the capital stack for a greenfield development project will require the developer guarantee the construction loan during construction and will often want to hold back a significant portion of the agreed upon developer fee until completion of the project.

In addition, the developer can expect a REIT or similar group to demand a greater percentage of the profits or *promote*—up to 100 percent in some cases. This is a very important point for the developer to consider. Are you willing to trade profit or *promote* in the project for risk mitigation and an easier path to the overall project financing?

9 LENDERS' LEGAL STRUCTURE

Since the lenders have a first lien position, they do everything they can to assure a position of legal priority. With this in mind, lenders often require that all the assets of a commercial real estate project all be owned by a *single purpose entity*. This requires that all the assets of the project, including the cash infused by the equity provider, land contract, architectural agreements and drawings and even tenant lease agreements, be assigned and contributed to a legal entity that conducts no other business than the project itself. The lender will then *perfect* his *first lien position* in the single purpose entity and the assets. The bank or lender can perfect its interest in a piece of real estate by filing evidence of this first lien with the land records at the courthouse in the county where the property for the project is located. A lien on *personal property*, on the other hand, like stock in the single purpose entity, cash, and accounts receivable is perfected by filing *UCC-1* with the secretary of state's office or taking physical possession of the property. A UCC-1 is a statutory filing process adopted in all fifty states and represents a uniform process for someone to announce to the world their rights in the claimed personal property. UCC stands for *Uniform Commercial Code.* Lenders and others like to focus their lending and collateral interest in a single purpose entity so that they can protect these assets from the creditors of the project including the originator—you, the developer! This priority and type of perfection in the single purpose entity is sometimes referred to as rendering the single-purpose entity, *bankruptcy remote.*

10 CONSTRUCTION DRAW OR FUNDING PROCESS

As discussed in the what section of the book construction loans typically work on a scheduled regular request for funds managed by the developer. The monthly request for funding is referred to as the *pay application or draw* request. The draw or pay application is the mechanism by which the construction lender is petitioned regularly, usually monthly and then reoccurring as the building is built. The draw to cover construction cost is compiled by the general contractor and the developer; it is used to pay the various expenses that were approved in the final budget at the time the project was under consideration. The complete project work product, from which the draw is based, is referred to as the *schedule of values (SoV)*.

The SoV is a detailed break out of the construction contract amount. Each draw request to the bank should utilize the SoV format. The SoV will typically consist of a description of each item to be paid and the budget for that item, current monthly budget request, and a rolling monthly budget total showing previous application and the percent the item is complete by the current draw request. Finally the SoV should set forth the applicable *retention amount*. Each draw should also include lien releases from everyone paid in the prior month's draw. Obtaining the lien releases from each of the subcontractors at the time of payment for their services performed in the prior period is extremely important to prevent the contractor or subcontractor from accruing or filing a possible *statutory lien*. Contractors and subcontractors have a legal right to get paid for the work they actually perform much like mechanics have a statutory right to paid after working on an automobile. Some lenders will require the developer bring down or *date down the title* on each draw to give them assurance that no such lien has been filed. This is called a *date-down endorsement,* and the process helps ensure against lien filings. It also indicates a way to reflect that the loan amount has increased. Finally, for each request for payment, the draw should include invoices and receipts that detail the reason for payment and these should match with the requested draw and SoV. Some draws will also contain construction change orders requests and summary. *Change orders* are discussed in detail in the *what* chapter.

11 LAND FINANCING

Acquiring the right to develop the land and or to purchase the land is often a separate loan process from the construction loan and will have different *loan-to-value* requirements, as well as different levels of commitment and diligence. This is sometimes referred to as the *land development loan or land loan.* A lender will normally loan no more than 50 percent of the land value when you are trying to finance the acquisition of a parcel of land. This is because at that point the development project is still speculative. However, it is acceptable to budget the land purchase or take the land financing out of the construction loan. From the lender's perspective this makes sense because when you are able to finance the construction of a project, there are committed tenants—the 50 percent preleasing we discussed earlier or you have demonstrated some form of guaranteed takeout of the construction loan. Thus the loan or debt portion of the capital stack appears to be much less speculative. The reason the loan appears less speculative and more stable when you have a *lease agreement* with tenants is that you have a predictable cash flow tied to a legally binding agreement. A predictable cash flow (signed legally binding lease agreement) allows an *appraiser* to *appraise* the property as income producing and *income producing* properties are inherently more valuable and, therefore, normally appraise at a higher value. A higher appraised value will enable you to borrow more money. This is another good reason to move the potential tenants to a full-blown lease agreement as soon as possible. It is the lease agreement that gives the appraiser assurance that the income method of evaluation is appropriate, and more importantly, the lender gets assurance the project can meet required interest coverage ratios and has a greater chance for success.

12 LAND AS EQUITY

Developers will often want to explore the possibility of partnering with a landowner by having the landowner contribute the land to a project. Assuming the land can be transferred *free of lien* the land would be considered equity by the lender. Of course, this would mean you have a new partner—the landowner. The landowner might contribute the property for the development because they are convinced the project represents the *highest and best use for* the property. Highest and best use is a real estate term related to appraisals. It implies that the value of a property is directly related to its use. The highest and best use therefore is one that will produce the greatest value. Lenders often look at the contribution of the land by the landowner favorably (some evidence that the landowner believes in the probable success of the project) but usually not so favorably as to reduce the overall equity they want to see for the project. Many lenders will also require cash infusion for equity above and beyond the land contribution so you may still need to raise additional cash.

Landowners often have a high expectation of the land value. In negotiating a transfer or value price for the land between the developer and the landowner, it can be helpful to rely on the appraisal. The appraisal will establish how much can be borrowed on the land and therefore how much equity the land represents to the capital stack of the project. Since the lender will only allow you to borrow a percentage of the appraised value, this represents a good starting place to discuss transfer value with the owner. However, the appraised value and market value, especially a landowner's perceived market value, are rarely equivalent. To bridge this difference in value, you will typically need to include the landowner in the development partnership and negotiate with the owner a profit participation in the development project.

13 THE MASTER SITE PLAN AND MULTIPLE PHASES

Many CRE developments contemplate numerous phases and even different product types in the same development. Often these different product types are built separately and or timed to be built separately. These development types require a *master site plan* and a well-considered vision related to the different phases, the timing of these phases, and the different issues associated with each phase and the product type and use.

Let us return to the sports bar and restaurant example and assume for a moment that the land parcel you have chosen consist of numerous acres, much more than needed for the sports bar and restaurant. The owner of the land parcel does not want to subdivide, and you need to purchase the entire tract. With the larger parcel you can now build a retail strip center behind the restaurant, and you have room for a free-standing bank or coffee shop on the opposite entrance corner across from the restaurant. With the introduction of a larger land parcel, phased construction, and multiple product types, there are numerous new wrinkles to consider related to the project.

Let us start with financing. (Surprise!) You have to purchase a large land parcel, more than what is needed for the sports bar and restaurant, and therefore now have to justify raising more money. You will need to demonstrate a potential for greater cash flow, which as we now know translates to more rent paying tenants. Of course, you believe the strip center as well as the bank or coffee house on the corner will translate to more rent paying tenants, and you plan to move forward. In a multi-phased project there will be greater *on- and off-site costs* associated with a larger parcel. With the introduction of a multiphased, multiproduct, master-plan-type development, you have greater up-front costs that make good sense for the overall project, but financing may be difficult to justify with the projected rental stream from phase one of the construction. A larger parcel creates site issues largely because there are many items like utilities, roadways, retention and other issues that require a greater investment up front regardless of the staging or timing of the phased development. You will for example probably want to clear the land and bring roads, parking, water, sewage, electric and other utilities to the entire sight not just to the sports bar and restaurant site. A multi phased master development effort requires significant planning, coordination and management between the numerous tenants and users. This coordination and management is typically organized by the developer in the *master declaration*. The master declaration is the document that will address numerous issues but typically addresses such items as *reciprocal easements, covenants, conditions and restrictions (CC+Rs)* The master declaration is extremely important to properly organize and manage the development effort. Expect the key or anchor tenants to require significant conditions and restrictions in the master declaration related to future potential tenants, signage and other approval rights. As the developer try to keep the future approval rights of tenants as simple as possible. Once tenants are moved in and operating their business they can lose sight of the importance of cooperating with the developer. Requests for simple approvals can add months to the process of adding new tenants to the master development.

14 SELLING PAD SITES

One way to help finance a master plan development other than preleasing to new tenants or raising more equity is to sell certain tracts of land, sometimes referred to as *out parcels* or *pad sites*. Many users such as banks, coffee shops, and fast food restaurants want to own their development site and therefore want to purchase a pad. Pads or out parcels are also ground leased by the owner or developed as a, *build to suit*. A build to suit is a predesigned structure that is built to the exact needs and desires of user or tenant. A build to suit often requires the developer to finance the construction. A *reverse build to suit* will require the future tenant or user finance the construction but still sign a term lease agreement with the developer. From the developer's perspective, selling some or all of the out parcels or pads is a great way to help pay for the larger up-front costs and still keep the project on track and financeable. Pads, if sold can be sold *fee simple* to the buyer. Fee simple just refers to the fact the purchaser of the pad is deeded the property parcel. Pricing the sale of a pad to a user is much like setting a net present value to a long-term lease. Since you are typically selling the pad fee simple you want to realize the same or similar profits in the sale that you would have realized had you built and leased the site. The *broker teaming partner* can help you determine the going rate for pad sites in the development area of the project. However whether a pad site is sold or ground leased pad owners are often still subject to the covenants, conditions and restriction of the master declaration. It is still important for the developer to make sure there is coordination and consistency through-out the development project.

Regardless of whether you plan to sell pads, focus on tenant leasing commitment, or raise additional equity, you will need to be prepared to demonstrate to the lender and equity provider that you have enough cash flow commitment during the construction and lease-up phases to meet required minimum financial standards and demands.

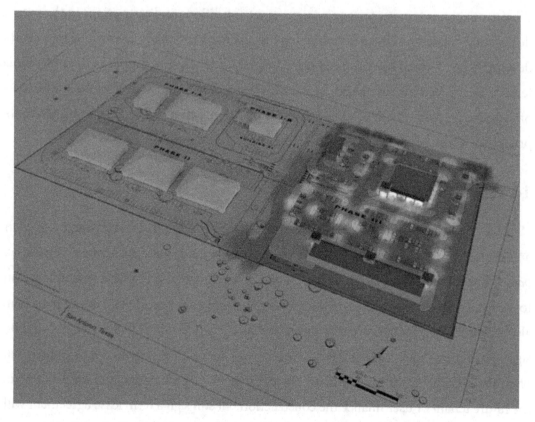

Table 1: Example of Master Site Plan with Multiple Phases
(5G Studio, Architects)

15 PURCHASING AND REFURBISHING EXISTING BUILDING

The true cost of purchasing an existing building or project not only includes the purchase price, but the cost of rehabbing and repairing the building and most importantly making the building suitable and attractive for the intended tenant and users (including tenant improvement allowance.) Since it is likely the developer knows the Sellers asking price it is important to focus on the estimated cost of rehab/repair and making the project suitable for the intended tenant and users. To adequately evaluate the rehab and repair issue the developer must make an inspection of the project. The initial inspection should include all aspects of the building including structural, systems (mechanical, electrical and plumbing), common area and exterior work. The goal of the initial inspection should be to identify any major issues that will make the rehab very expensive or extremely difficult.

To complete the assessment the developer must still consider two other major cost issues; making the space suitable for the tenant and tenant improvement cost. Making the project suitable for tenants represents costs that the developer may need to occur to attract tenants but may not be investments that are not tied to any specific tenant or user. Benefits and features that are required or important to attract tenants can typically be determined by knowing the regulatory requirements and exploring comparable projects and buildings in the area. For example if you are looking to purchase and rehab a building for medical use it is important to understand requirement of the intended user. Medical buildings require larger elevators, larger doors and hallways, handicap accessible bathrooms and other unique features.

The developer must also consider tenant improvement cost. Tenant improvement costs are costs that the developer will pay to entice the tenant user to the building. Tenant Improvement cost or the developer "TI" allowance can be very expensive and add substantial investment to a project. It is important that the developer adequately research the TI allowance made available by other landlords in the surrounding market so the project lease terms are competitive with nearby buildings. The developer should be able to learn the typical TI allowance for comparable buildings and projects from the real estate broker teaming partner. Finally, it is important for the developer to clearly define where the building core and shell ends and the tenant TI begins. With this in mind early in the process the developer should have the architect or contractor create a working specifications document that clearly defines how the developer will deliver the tenant space and therefore define what will be considered tenant improvement.

Understanding these three important costs will help guide the developer in evaluating the major issues related to purchasing and rehabbing an existing commercial building Moreover it will help the developer determine if the investment makes good economic sense. Ultimately, the overall investment must make good economic sense; translate to competitive lease terms for the intended tenants and an attractive return for the developer.

16 CONSTRUCTION LOAN: MARKETING BASICS

Let us explore the sports bar and restaurant concept to demonstrate certain marketing basics. Let us assume for a moment that you have been negotiating with a current restaurant owner/operator who would like to expand to the site you have selected for the development project. Since the potential tenant is an existing restaurant owner let us start there. The future potential tenant has an existing restaurant and bar so let us assume he wants the image and brand for the new facility to be substantially similar to the existing facility. He will have likely worked with an architect to develop the first site. Working with the original architect you can develop an *initial site plan* for the new development. The initial site plan is the architect's attempt at taking the conceptual building outline and placing it on the site you have chosen. Now, having had designed and developed the original restaurant the architect can work up a drawing of how the building might look sometimes referred to as a *rendering*.

Now let us take a quick inventory of how the initial project plan can come together and help you begin presenting to and selling the concept to possible construction lenders. First we have a potential tenant with an existing business. Existing businesses have location, revenue, financials, customers, competition, suppliers, etc. We have a rendering and a site plan from an experienced architect (possible teaming partner) that shows how the current concept can be expanded to the new site. We have a preliminary site that we can initially map, showing the site, surrounding items of interest, other restaurants, and competition, and big-box retailers. We have collected facts on the surrounding population from the Internet or from the city's own Web site. Finally we have information about you that is important you are the developer.

As the developer, you need to take all the information mentioned above and more and put it together in a presentation format that you are comfortable with and begin marketing the project plan and vision. It is time to confront not only the construction lender we have been talking about but also the remaining players in raising the capital stack—the equity investors.

Table 2: Strip Center, Restaurant, and Sports Bar Rendering
(5G Studio, Architects)

CHAPTER 12: EQUITY INVESTOR

INTRODUCTION

If the debt component of a projected cost is 65-75 percent of the amount of money needed to get a project built, where does the remaining 25-35 percent come from? This remaining portion of the *capital stack* is typically referred to as *equity*. ➡ Equity is cash or the equivalent of cash (land) invested in a project that is the *first money* invested and *subordinated* to the bank or construction lender that has supplied the construction loan. In this context, *subordinated* means that the bank or lender has a *priority or first lien position* on the assets of the project and the equity investor can only take a second lien. Thus a subordinated interest is behind the bank and project creditors in the assets of the project. Equity investors are typically first in, last out when it comes to the cash distribution.

Equity can come from many sources. The equity might very well be the land the project is to be built on or cash invested by friends and family members. Equity also comes from more traditional market-driven sources such as wealthy third-party individuals, investment firms, and pension funds. Of course, if you have the capability, equity can always come from you, the developer. ➡ For purposes of this book, we are assuming that the equity is coming from a third party, unrelated market-driven source such as pension fund or investment group that specializes in investing in new real estate development projects. Utilizing a third-party investor as our guide forces the developer to ask and answer all the key questions and issues as we touched on in the introduction to this book.

1 EQUITY INVESTMENT PROCESS

Early in the predevelopment process you will want to get an indication of interest from the potential equity provider. You will do this with potential equity investors in much the same way as outlined in the previous chapter for the construction lender. The first goal is to enter into an LOI that indicates a strong interest to invest. To obtain the LOI, you must supply the equity investor with specific information related to the project that meets the initial *underwriting criteria* of the equity investor. Like the lender, the equity term sheet or LOI is nonbinding and subject to ongoing due diligence, specific approvals, and final documentation. As the deal progresses you may get the equity investor to issue a *commitment letter*. The commitment letter is a slightly stronger indication of interest by the investor group that they will make the equity investment contemplated under the terms and conditions outlined in the letter. The equity investor, like the lender, is also likely to charge some form of due diligence fee and origination fee, and may also want to charge an ongoing management fee to oversee the development effort as it progresses. ➡ Regardless of the fees the equity provider may charge, the developer is responsible for reimbursing all out-of-pocket costs and expenses of the equity investor and debt provider in reviewing the request for investment or loan.

2 THE EQUITY INVESTOR AND RETURN ON INVESTMENT

Since equity investors are subordinating their investment to the bank (debt), they are in a riskier position with regards to reimbursement and receiving a return on their investment. You will find that while the lender seems to focus on getting his principal repaid with an interest payment, the equity investor is much more focused on getting a significant return for his investment. Since equity investors take more risk, i.e., they are subordinated to the lender and the costs of the project, they demand a greater return on their investment. Equity investors will typically look to get their money back along with a *preferred return or pref* (earned interest). It is referred to as a pref or preference because the holder gets paid this interest before certain others (like the developer) get paid. In addition to return of their principal investment and a pref, equity investors typically expect a significant amount of the profit or promote upon sale of the project. The equity investor gets paid out of proceeds that exceed the monies owed to the lender and the expenses of the project. It is only after the lender is paid off and all expenses, including expenses of sale of the project, are covered that the equity investors get their preferred return, their investment, and participate in the profits, if any. The flow or stream of the cash generated from profits of a project from the perspective of the investor group is often referred to as the *waterfall*. It is referred to as the waterfall because of the cascading effect of the distribution of cash proceeds or profits when there is an event that creates cash There are basically ➡ two types of equity investors developers need to consider when looking for equity investment in a green build, income producing, real estate development project—short or long term. The short-term equity investor will want to realize his return about the time the construction loan expires and needs to be refinanced, therefore realizing the return on investment in probably five years or less. The long-term equity investor invests assuming the invested money will stay in the project for a longer period of time, often ten years or more. The REITS we discussed earlier in the construction debt chapter are a good example of investors that typically hold the property for a longer term. A long-term investor will typically finance the entire capital stack from the beginning of the project or will price into the overall cost of the project taking the lender out at or before construction loan maturity. We focus on the short-term investor for this book because the developer is responsible for finding and closing on the construction debt. Most short-term equity investors for a start-up or *greenfield* development project expect ROI in the 20 percent range. Since they are receiving their return in a shorter period of time (and the developer has arranged for the construction debt financing) they are typically open to splitting a large portion of the profits with the developer (up to 50 percent see discussion in the why section of the book).. As discussed in the previous chapter on one-stop-shop lender, a developer brings less value to the project if the equity investor supplies the entire capital stack and therefore the profit participation (along with the developer risk) is greatly reduced.

3 ROI, IRR, AND THE TIME VALUE OF MONEY

Most equity investors are guided by a couple of fundamental investment concepts. One of these we discuss in the why section—the concept of *minimizing risk and maximizing return*. There are a couple of other concepts that are worth addressing and that developers need to understand as they present the development vision and project plan. First, the *time value of money*—what kind of return will the investor get over the amount of time the money is tied up in the project? Second, what is an acceptable rate of return the investor will be willing to assume for investing his money?

To understand the concepts of the time value of money and an acceptable rate of return, ask yourself, why would someone want to invest money to build a new CRE development project, and what would make this investment a good one? In a general sense there are not that many components to consider. You, the developer will take the money and use it to get more money from the lender. With this available money, you will buy the land, build the building, fill it with tenants, manage the operation, and then either manage long term or sell the finished project. The equity investor will evaluate the risk associated with each of these steps, estimate how long it will take to complete, forecast the net cash flow, and then estimate how much a buyer will pay for the finished product. ➡ If you take the following components: how much money is invested, how long the money is invested, what is the cash flow received during the investment period, how much profit might be realized upon sale of the property and throw them into a formula and add a *yield*, you can determine the *internal rate of return* (IRR) and the *return on Investment* (ROI). The ROI is a way for investors to measure the profitability of a real estate investment while the IRR helps provide an estimate of the future return on investment. As mentioned earlier, most equity investors for a start-up or *greenfield* development project expect ROI in the 20 percent range; more about this concept in the why section. A developer also needs to be aware of the investor's *cash-on-cash return*. Calculating a cash-on-cash return for a property is a way of calculating the ROI in relation to the investor's out-of-pocket cash. The cash-on-cash return for a real estate investment relates pretax annual cash received to cash actually invested; it is stated as a percentage. ➡ One additional caveat that's probably related to the minimize risk, maximize return investment principle, most institutional equity investors want to see the developer put cash in the development project. The project equity investor will typically expect the developer to put up 5-10 percent of the total equity investment needed. This is often referred to as *skin in the game* or what this guide refers to as the *developer coinvestment*.

4 THE DEVELOPER COINVESTMENT

The developer coinvestment is as important to the equity investor as the personal guarantee is to the lender. This coinvestment can often be a large sum of money, and if you are a new developer or even an experienced developer, you may not have this kind of cash on hand and ready to invest. The good news is that in many cases you can get the equity investor to allow you to contribute a portion of the developer fee as the developer coinvestment.

The amount and timing of the developer coinvestment can and should be discussed and negotiated with the equity investor and lender. It is typically in the developer's best interest to minimize the developer coinvestment amount if the developer profit participation is not affected. If you can demonstrate to the potential equity investor that you have minimized his risk in some substantial way, i.e., you have preleased over 70 percent of the project (rather than the 50 percent referred to earlier) or you have only 50 percent preleased but a very substantial parent company of the tenant is going to guarantee the lease agreement. If you plan to utilize the developer fee for the developer coinvestment, try to retain a significant portion of the developer fee for distribution during construction. There is a lot of work left to do and keeping a portion of the fee will allow you to receive some cash during construction.

5 DEVELOPER FEE CAVEATS

If you plan to utilize the developer fee as the developer coinvestment, consult with the team lawyer or tax adviser about the tax consequences of contributing a portion of the fee. For federal and state income tax purposes, you may be deemed to have received the fee by investing it although you may not have actually received it. This may mean you owe taxes on the portion of the developer fee you utilize for the developer coinvestment amount. This can create a real cash flow problem come tax time. There are ways to utilize the fee as the coinvestment and postpone tax due. This is most often achieved by having the developer coinvestment portion of the developer fee be earned only upon meeting certain goals and objectives of the project. In this instance the full fee is budgeted and approved but only earned and payable upon meeting certain goals like substantial completion of construction or issuance of the *certificate of occupancy* for the building(s). Once earned and payable, it is converted or transferred to the developer coinvestment or equity contribution account. It is important to discuss this issue with the lender and equity provider so that the legal documents properly reflect the mechanics. This issue is beyond the scope of this book and should be discussed with the project legal counsel and tax advisers.

One final point: the developer coinvestment or equity contribution should be treated the same or equal to the equity investors capital investment. In other words the developers investment should be treated *pari passu* to the equity investors, investment. Pari passu is a Latin term that means at an equal rate or pace. In the context of a development project, pari passu conveys that if and when there are proceeds or profit upon the sale of the project, the developer is paid at the same time and with the same return as the equity investor. Remember the waterfall we discussed in an earlier chapter? Of course, equity investors do not always see it that way and sometimes want to build in a minimum return before the developer can participate. This minimum return is sometimes referred to as a *lookback* or *clawback*. Just the name clawback should tell you a little about the concept! A lookback or clawback assures the equity investor a certain minimum level of return on his money before the developer gets to participate in the profit or promote. Remember the concept of first in, last out that we discussed earlier. Most equity investors agree to apply the clawback principle only to profits and not to the pref or the invested equity. The lookback or clawback is one way the equity investor offers the developer the privilege of being the last out. The good news is once the equity investor get the negotiated lookback or clawback level of return, the developer (you) should be able to structure the deal so that he catches up with the remaining profits; excess profits (if any) are typically split equally.

6 THE DEVELOPER AS A TENANT

There may come a time in the predevelopment stage when the project has moved forward and is very close to being complete, but you don't quite have the preleasing needed or the equity investor or even debt provider are looking for one more element to assure them that this deal makes economic sense. In this event, ➡ you, as the developer, might actually need to enter into a lease agreement for space in the project! Yes, you might need to sign a lease agreement for space in the building. Equity investors and debt providers will often allow you to rent space in the project by signing a legally binding lease agreement. This is to ensure that the building will be adequately leased up and the debt and equity are comfortable with the overall cash flow projections. The lease agreement is typically under the same terms and conditions outlined in the project budget and pro forma, i.e., the developer is held to the standards set forth in the projections for third-party tenants, except, of course, for the tenant improvement allowance (TI). You should not need TI if you don't plan on moving in. This is sometimes referred to as *bootstrapping* by the debt or equity. The developer's lease agreement, if there is one, is negotiated and entered into before funding and is usually triggered by failing to meet specified cash flow projections or certain financial ratios at a point in time after building completion. This is also referred to as developer incentive— incentive to get the project leased up, tenants moved into the building, and rent coming in.

7 MEZZANINE FINANCING

You may recall earlier in this chapter we discussed the project equity. *"If the debt component of a projected cost is 65-75 percent of the amount of money needed to get a project built, where does the remaining 25-35 percent come from? This remaining portion of the capital stack is typically referred to as equity. (Note the land as equity discussion above.) Equity is cash or the equivalent of cash (land) invested in a project that is the first money invested and subordinated to the bank that has supplied the construction loan."* However 25-35 percent of the project cost can often be a large amount of money. In many development projects this amounts to millions or even tens of millions of dollars. Often developers of projects will obtain a *mezzanine loan* to help bridge the large difference between the debt and equity component of the capital stack. The mezzanine lender is subordinated to the interest of the construction lender but will often attempt to perfect a position in the ownership of the single purpose entity or company that owns the development and property. Typically, this is accomplished by the single purpose entity assigning the company stock to the mezzanine lender. The logic being that if the developer creates or causes an event of default under the construction loan the mezzanine lender can quickly step into the shoes of the developer by exercising his rights to the assigned stock of the company. With the stock in hand, the mezzanine lender can take over managing the development and do what is necessary to keep the construction lender from foreclosing. Mezzanine lenders will typically seek a double-digit interest rate, *points* for making the loan, and participation in the developer *profit, or upside* to the development effort. Developers who can utilize the land as equity often look to a mezzanine-type loan structure to complete the equity component of the capital stack. Utilizing a mezzanine lender and not a third-party equity investor to complete the capital stack may result in a greater profit or promote percentage to the developer. Since mezzanine investors are somewhat secured and receive a higher interest rate, they receive a smaller percentage of the promote or profits percentage.

8 THE EQUITY INVESTOR LEGAL STRUCTURE

To document the investment, equity investors typically require a *limited partnership* be formed between the developer and an entity the equity investor forms for this investment project (in many states equity investors prefer limited liability companies. You should discuss with counsel what is the preferred vehicle in your state. The partnership will be run by a *general partner* or *GP* typically controlled by…surprise—you, the developer. However, the partnership document generally required by the equity investor will outline in very specific terms the powers of the GP and when the GP must seek approval from the limited partners. Equity investors also typically require a *development or management agreement* that outlines the performance obligations expected of the developer by the equity investor for the project. The performance obligations typically track what you previously outlined in the in the *project plan.* ➡ This is an important point to understand. The project plan is not only the primary sales and marketing tool for the project but also represents the start of negotiation with the investors, more about this in the why section. ➡ Finally, you may be asked to guarantee certain performance obligations set forth in the development agreement. Like the debt provider, the equity investor is also likely to require some form of environmental indemnity and even *take out provisions*. Take out provisions require the developer to buy out or take out the investment by the equity investor if the project doesn't perform as planned. Performance obligations, environmental indemnities, and even take out provisions are very good reasons to line up the right equity investor teaming partners for the project.

9 THE EQUITY INVESTOR UNDERWRITING CRITERIA

The process both the lender and equity investor go through internally as they review the project plan is often referred to as the *underwriting*. To fulfill the needs and requirements of the underwriting, a lender and equity investor will conduct *due diligence*. Due diligence will vary depending on the project to be developed but will generally involve a detailed look at the who, what, where, and why variables that we explore in detail throughout this book.

Most equity investors view potential investment in three stages: *underwriting, approvals, and funding.* Each of these stages has significant due diligence activity that must be completed to move on to the next stage and ultimately complete the process. In addition, each stage of due diligence tends to move simultaneously so that all the necessary components come together at the same time. As you read this book, you will see how each of the stages fit into the overall scheme of how to get a project financed and built.

LIST OF TYPICAL KEY DILIGENCE ITEMS FOR EQUITY INVESTMENT:

UNDERWRITING: Location of Property, Development Budget, Construction Period and Timetable, Construction Debt Assumptions, Pro Forma Rent Roll and Lease Up, Pre Leasing Update and Tenant Terms, Tenant Letters of Intent.

APPROVALS: Site Plan, Renderings of Buildings, Schematic Design Documents, Information and Status of Environmental Issues-Phase I, Land Sales Comparables, Sales Comparables, Lease Comparables, Map with Location and Competition.

FUNDING DOCUMENTATION: Partnership Agreement, Purchase and Sale Agreement, Loan Commitment Letter, Development and Construction Schedule, ALTA Survey, Environmental Phase I, Geotechnical Report, General Contractor Contract, AIA Contract for Architect, Construction Drawings, Evidence of Building Permit, Zoning and Development rights, Appraisal of Land to be Developed, Executed Tenant Leases, LOI's, Commitment for Title Insurance, Evidence of Insurance for Property, Loan Documents, Management Agreement.

Index